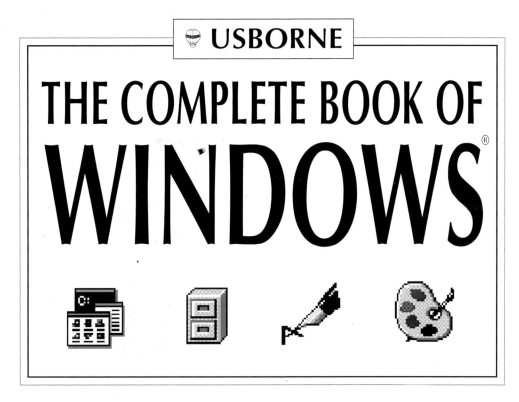

USBORNE

THE COMPLETE BOOK OF
WINDOWS®

WINDOWS FOR BEGINNERS
page 1

PROJECTS FOR WINDOWS
FOR BEGINNERS
page 49

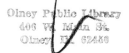

WINDOWS®
FOR BEGINNERS

Richard Dungworth

Edited by Philippa Wingate

Editorial consultants: Jane Chisholm & Anthony Marks

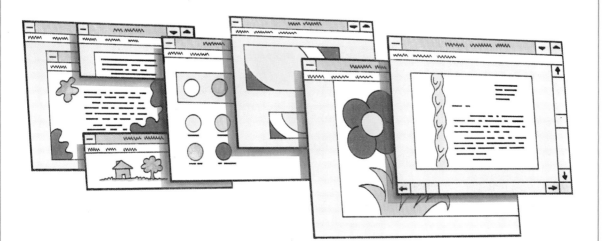

Designed by Neil Francis & Steve Page

Additional designs by Sarah Bealham, Non Figg & Russell Punter

Illustrated by Colin Mier, Derek Matthews, Andy Burton, Pete Taylor and Paul Southcombe

Technical Consultant: Richard Payne

Contents

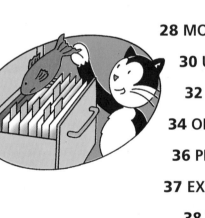

Introducing Microsoft Windows

You can use your personal computer, or PC, for all sorts of amazing jobs. But before it can perform even the simplest task, your PC needs a list of instructions, called a program. To make sure that your computer has all the instructions it needs, you can buy whole sets of programs, grouped together as software.

Your computer needs software before it can work.

What is Microsoft Windows?

Microsoft® Windows® is a special piece of software which enables you to tell your PC what you want it to do. You use Windows to control all the other software on your computer. This section of the book explains the simple techniques you'll need to become one of the 80 million people who use Windows to control their PC.

Windows lets you control your PC quickly and easily.

Windows versions

From time to time Microsoft brings out a new version of the Windows system.The new version includes various improvements on earlier versions. Each Windows version is given a number. The higher the number, the more recent the version.

This section of the book concentrates on version 3.1 of the Windows software. Its screen pictures show the Windows® 3.1 display. But you can use the same techniques to operate other versions of Windows, including Windows® 3.11.

Windows 95

The most advanced version of Microsoft Windows is called Windows® 95. You can find out more about the Windows® 95 system on pages 46 & 47.

About this section

This section of the book introduces all the main features of Windows, telling you how to use them step-by-step. The first time you read it, work through page by page from beginning to end. Later, you can use the index at the back of the book to look up particular topics to refresh your memory.

Getting help

Some pages include "help" boxes with a lifebelt in the top left-hand corner. These boxes contain tips to help you cope as you find your way around Windows.

If you need extra help, you can find out on pages 44 and 45 how to use the instructions that are included in the Windows software.

DOS, Windows and applications

In order to work properly, a computer needs a piece of software called an operating system. One of an operating system's main jobs is to take in commands from the person using the computer (known as the user) and convert them into instructions which the computer can understand.

MS-DOS

Most personal computers use an operating system called Microsoft Disk Operating System. It is known as MS-DOS or DOS for short. With DOS, you tell your computer what to do by typing in command codes using your PC's keyboard. Some DOS commands are somewhat complicated.

To make DOS easier to use, Microsoft developed the Windows system. Windows works with DOS to enable you to control your computer without having to type in DOS commands.

How does Windows work?

The Windows system fills your PC's display with pictures. By "touching" or moving these pictures in a particular way, using an on-screen pointer, you can tell Windows what you want your computer to do. Windows then controls DOS on your behalf to make your computer carry out your commands.

This screen shows the Windows display.

You will find out about the different pictures which make up the Windows display on pages 8 and 9.

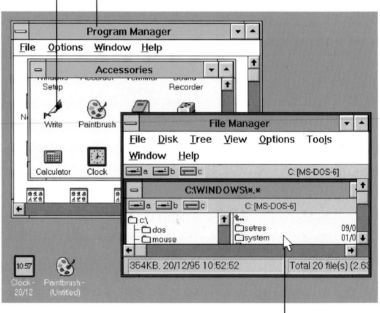

This pointer enables you to touch specific parts of the display.

Mouse control

Instead of using your computer's keyboard to control the Windows pointer, you move it around using a hand-held device, connected to the computer by a thin cable. Because of its shape and its cable "tail", this gadget is known as a mouse.

You will find out how to use your computer's mouse on pages 10 and 11 of this book.

Application software

Windows enables your PC to use, or "run", other pieces of software, called applications. Each application includes the instructions and information that your computer needs to play a particular role.

You can buy applications for a remarkable range of jobs. Games, drawing programs, and so-called spreadsheets and databases are all examples of applications. The picture below shows some of the things you can do with your PC by running applications.

Produce film

Work with text

Draw and design

Make music

Compatibility

When you buy an application to use with Windows on your PC, you must make sure that it is designed to be controlled with Windows, rather than with another operating system. Applications which work with the Windows system are said to be Windows compatible.

What you need to begin

To use Windows, you need a PC which can run the Windows software. Windows and its applications were originally designed for use on computers built by a company called IBM. But many other companies now sell PCs which are "IBM compatible", and can use the Windows system.

Some computers which run Windows are small enough to fit on your lap.

Installing Windows

Most PCs already have DOS and Windows software when you buy them. If yours doesn't, you need to buy the software and feed it into your PC. This is known as installing the software. Follow the installation instructions that are included with the software.

Standard applications

The applications used in this book to introduce Windows techniques are included in the Windows software when you buy it. So you don't need to buy any extra software to start learning.

You will find out on pages 16-21 how to use an application called Write to create a letter to a friend.

Pages 26-29 explain how you can use the Paintbrush application to draw pictures.

Starting and stopping

Before you can use Windows, you need to switch on your computer, and start the Windows software running.

Switching on

To switch on your computer, press its power switch. You also need to switch on the piece of equipment that shows your PC's display, called a monitor. Some monitors automatically come on when the computer that they're connected to is switched on, but others have a separate on/off switch.

Your computer will begin to make whirring noises. Long lists of command codes will begin to scroll up your screen. If this doesn't happen, check that all the power cords are plugged in correctly.

Running Windows

Once your computer is switched on, you need to make sure that the Windows software is running. Most computers which use Windows either automatically run the Windows software as they are switched on, or start up in DOS (see page 4).

If your PC is set to run the Windows software automatically, your screen will briefly show a picture of a multicolored flag (the Windows logo) before filling with the Windows display.

If your computer starts in DOS, the "DOS prompt", shown below, will appear on your screen.

The DOS prompt

In this case you need to start Windows running yourself. Type the letters WIN and press the **Return** key. The Windows logo and display will then appear on your screen.

Keystroke commands

As you work through this book, you will occasionally need to use your computer's keyboard to enter a command. This is known as using keystrokes. The keystrokes included in this book are printed in bold type, **like this**. Although keyboards vary, the diagram below should help you find the keys you need.

This diagram shows the typical layout of a PC's keyboard.

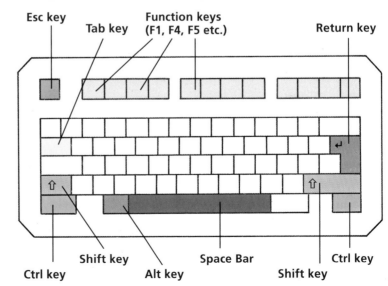

Esc key
Tab key
Function keys (F1, F4, F5 etc.)
Return key
Ctrl key
Shift key
Alt key
Space Bar
Ctrl key
Shift key

Computer health

Once you have successfully started Windows running, you can find out how to use it by working through the rest of this book. However, long periods of computing may damage your health. So, as you work with your P.C, it is important to take a break at least once an hour. When you take a short break, you can leave your computer switched on.

Screen savers

Don't be alarmed if you return after a break to find an unusual screen display. A monitor's screen can be damaged by showing the same image for a long time. So Windows often puts a moving "screen saver" on display if your mouse and keyboard are left untouched for a while.

The Windows display will return as soon as you give your mouse a nudge.

This screen shows an example of a Windows screen saver.

HELP!

When you disturb a screen saver, a box like the one below may appear on your screen. This means that the screen saver is "locked" on. To return to the Windows display you will need to ask the person who set this lock for their screen saver password.

Flying Window

(!) The screen saver you are using is password protected. You must type in the screen saver password to turn off the screen saver.

Password: [   ]

[OK]   [Cancel]

Shutting down

Another important thing to know is how to stop when you've finished using Windows for the day. This is known as shutting down.

Before you switch off your PC's power supply, you must bring your Windows session to an end. Switching off the power while Windows is still running can damage your computer.

Ending your session

When you are ready to shut down, follow the steps below to bring your Windows session to an end:

1 - Make sure that you have selected the part of the Windows system called Program Manager. You will find out how to do this on page 9.

2 - While holding down the **Alt** key, press the **F4** key. Release both keys.

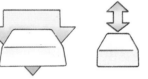

3 - The box shown below will appear on your screen. If you have changed your mind about stopping, press and release the **Esc** key. Otherwise press and release the **Return** key.

Exit Windows

(i) **This will end your Windows session.**

[OK]   [Cancel]

As Windows stops running, its display will vanish from the screen, and your computer will return to DOS. Once the DOS prompt appears, you can safely switch off your PC and its monitor.

The Windows desktop

Once Windows is running, it fills your screen with a display called the desktop. Your desktop may be almost empty to begin with, but as you work with Windows, it will become crowded with pictures, like the example shown on the right. These pages introduce the main parts of the Windows desktop.

Programs and pictures

Just like an ordinary desk, a busy Windows desktop is scattered with useful items. But instead of providing a real notepad, calculator, address book, or clock, Windows spreads out programs that do the same jobs as these articles. Each picture on the desktop represents one of these programs. There are two main types of desktop pictures, called windows and icons.

This screen shows a crowded Windows desktop.

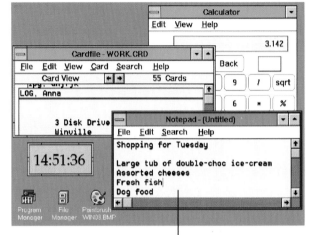

When an item on the Windows desktop overlaps others, it is described as being nearer to the top of the desktop.

What is a window?

A window is a rectangular box, with a thin border on all four sides, and a thicker strip across its top edge. The picture below shows what a typical window looks like, and what its various parts are called. You will find out on pages 12 and 13 what a window's borders, buttons and bars are for.

A window

This small square with a slot in it is called a control-menu box.

This strip across the top edge of a window is called a title bar.

Most windows have a second strip containing a row of words. This is called a menu bar.

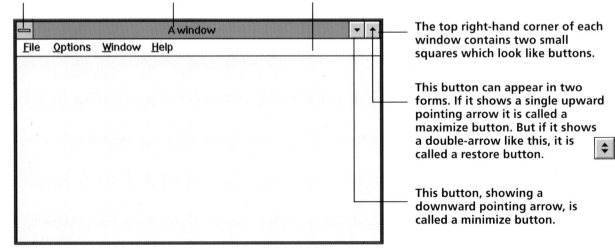

The top right-hand corner of each window contains two small squares which look like buttons.

This button can appear in two forms. If it shows a single upward pointing arrow it is called a maximize button. But if it shows a double-arrow like this, it is called a restore button.

This button, showing a downward pointing arrow, is called a minimize button.

Icons

Instead of appearing as a window, a program can be represented on the desktop by a small picture, called an icon. Icons can appear anywhere on your desktop. They are often found along the bottom edge of your screen.

An icon usually has a label underneath it, giving the name of the program it represents.

These are some of the icons that you will come across on your Windows desktop.

File Manager   Paintbrush   Clock   Calculator

Write   Notepad   Cardfile   Calendar

The appearance of a program's icon often provides a clue to what that program is for. For example, the icon for Paintbrush, a program which lets you draw pictures, looks like an artist's paint palette and brush.

The pointer

Somewhere on your desktop you'll find the pointer (see page 4). The pointer usually appears as a small arrowhead, but depending on what you are using it for, it can take on any of the forms shown below.

The arrowhead pointer   *Other pointer shapes*

Wallpaper

The Windows desktop is sometimes decorated with a patterned layer, called wallpaper. There are lots of different designs of desktop wallpaper.

This screen shows an example of Windows wallpaper.

Finding Program Manager

On the next two pages of this book you will find out how to use your mouse to control the Windows desktop. You'll use a window called Program Manager for this mouse practice, so you need to make sure that the Program Manager window is on top of your desktop.

Hold down the **Alt** key. When you press and release the **Tab** key, a box containing an icon and its name will appear in the middle of your screen. If the icon and name are different from those shown in the box below, keep the **Alt** key held down and press and release the **Tab** key again. Keep doing this until the box shows Program Manager's icon and name as shown below.

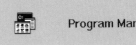

Program Manager

Now release the **Alt** key and the Program Manager window will jump to the top of your desktop. To make sure the window fills your screen, hold down the **Alt** key and press the **Space Bar**. Release both keys, and type the letter **X**.

You'll find out more about Program Manager on pages 14 and 15.

Using your mouse

Now that you know what the Windows desktop looks like, you can find out how to use it to tell your computer what to do.

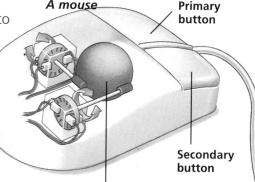

A mouse

Primary button

Secondary button

As you move the mouse, the motion of this ball is converted into movement of the pointer across your screen.

Pointing things out

To operate the desktop, you use the on-screen pointer as an electronic finger to pick out and move around specific parts of the display. You control the pointer's movements using a mouse (see page 4). The picture on the right shows a computer mouse, cut away so that you can see inside.

Most mice have two switches on their top surface, called the primary and secondary mouse buttons. The primary button is usually on the left, as shown in the picture. But if your computer is set for a left-handed mouse user, the buttons switch positions.

Mouse movements

Try moving your mouse around on a flat, clean surface. The pointer will follow your mouse movements by moving across the screen.

This is how you hold your mouse.

Use a special mouse mat if you have one, but a hardback book or a clear area of desk will do.

If your mouse reaches the edge of the surface that you're using it on, lift it up and replace it near the middle of the surface. By lifting your mouse, you can reposition it on your work surface without altering the position of the pointer on your screen. Use this technique to make the space you need to move your mouse in the direction you want.

Clicking

To "touch" part of the display, use your mouse to move the pointer over it, and then press and release the primary mouse button (see above). This is called clicking. It is the main way in which you use your mouse to control Windows.

You can click on various things on the desktop, some of which look like buttons. Try clicking on the restore button in the top right-hand corner of Program Manager's window on your screen (see page 8). Clicking on this button will cause the window

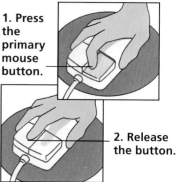

Clicking

1. Press the primary mouse button.

2. Release the button.

to shrink so that it covers only part of the desktop, rather than filling the whole screen.

'Click'   'Click'   'Click'

Dragging

To move something around on the desktop, you use another mouse technique, called dragging.

Position the pointer over the item you want to move. Press and hold down the primary mouse button. Imagine that you are grabbing and holding on to the item. By keeping the primary button depressed as you move your mouse, you can drag the item to another area of the desktop. Once it is where you want it, release the mouse button to drop the item into its new desktop location.

Try out your dragging technique by moving the Program Manager window to a new position on your desktop. To move the window, drag its title bar.

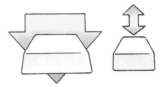

Using your mouse to drag

Press down the primary mouse button.

Hold down the button as you move the mouse.

Release the mouse button.

Double-clicking

The final mouse technique is called double-clicking. This is a special way of touching an item on the desktop. To double-click on part of your display, move the pointer over it and press and release the primary mouse button twice in quick succession.

Double-clicking usually offers a shortcut way to do something. For example, double-clicking on a window's title bar provides a speedy way to change the window's size. Try out your double-click on the Program Manager window's title bar.

Mouse lessons

To improve your mouse skills, you can use a lesson which is included in the Windows software. This is how you start the lesson:

1 - Make sure that the Program Manager window is selected (see page 9).

2 - While holding down the **Alt** key, type the letter **H**. Release both keys.

3 - Type the letter **W**.

Now follow the instructions which appear on your screen to use the Mouse Lesson. When you have had enough mouse practice, press the **Esc** key to return to the desktop display.

'Click'
'Click'

HELP!

If you lose sight of Program Manager as you try out your mouse skills, you can bring it back to the top of your desktop using the **Alt** and **Tab** keys (see page 9). You'll find out more about how to find things on your Windows desktop on pages 40 & 41.

Controlling a window

A window provides a workspace on your desktop in which you can use a particular program. Now that you can click, drag and double-click, you need to know how to use these mouse skills to control a typical window, so that you can work with Windows programs.

Open windows

Windows that appear on your desktop are said to be open. Your computer can run several programs at the same time, so several windows can be open on the desktop. However, you can only use one of these open windows at a time.

Active or inactive?

When a particular window is in use it is known as the active window. It lies on top of the other "inactive" windows on your desktop, and usually has a different colored title bar.

When you want to use a specific window, you can make it active by clicking on any part of it. If you can't do this because the window is hidden by other items on your desktop, you will need to use one of the techniques described on pages 40 and 41 to "switch" to the window that you want to use.

A busy desktop

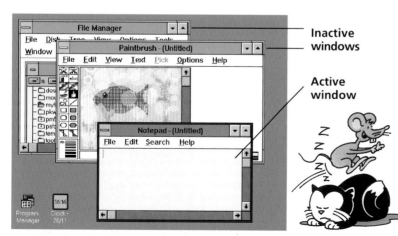

Inactive windows

Active window

Minimizing

If your desktop gets crowded with open windows, you can make some space by reducing the amount of room taken up by windows that you're not currently working with. By clicking on the minimize button in the top right-hand corner of a window, you can reduce that window to an icon at the bottom of your screen. This is known as minimizing a window.

Minimizing lets you put a program to one side for the time being. If you want to use that program again, you can convert its icon back into a window by double-clicking on it. Returning a window to its original size and location on your desktop is known as restoring that window.

Minimizing and restoring

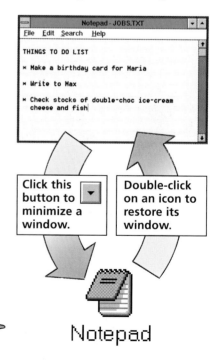

Click this button to minimize a window.

Double-click on an icon to restore its window.

Notepad

Maximizing

If you want more space inside a particular window, you can expand it so that it fills your screen. To do this, click on the window's maximize button.

A window which has been maximized fills the entire screen and has no surrounding border. Instead of a maximize button it has a restore button. You can return the window to its previous size and position by clicking this restore button.

Maximizing and restoring

Click this button to maximize a window.	Click this button to restore a window.

Moving a window

Unless it has been maximized to fill the screen, you can move a window around the desktop by dragging its title bar to a new location.

Changing a window's size

You can adjust the size of a window, stretching or shrinking it to make it wider, narrower, taller or shorter. To alter a window's size, point to the border that you want to move. The pointer will change into a double-headed arrow, showing the directions in which you can alter the window's shape. Hold down the mouse button and drag the border to a new position.

This diagram shows you the different ways in which you can change a window's size.

Drag the top or bottom border, using this shaped pointer, to make a window taller or shorter.

Drag a side border, using this shaped pointer, to make a window wider or narrower.

Drag a corner part of the border, using this shaped pointer, to adjust both the window's height and width.

Using scroll bars

Sometimes a window isn't big enough to display all its contents. When this is the case, the window has a "scroll bar" along its right edge, its bottom edge, or both these edges. You can use these scroll bars to shift the window's view so that you can look at any part of its contents.

To move your view a little at a time, click on the arrow button at either end of a scroll bar. To shift your view by a whole window size, click on the scroll bar itself. Or you can drag the small square called the scroll box along the scroll bar until the window shows the area you want.

A window with scroll bars

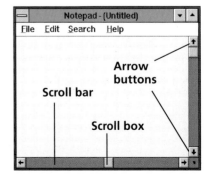

Arrow buttons

Scroll bar

Scroll box

Program Manager

To use a Windows program, you need to open its window on your desktop by running that program.

These pages introduce Program Manager, the part of the Windows system that lets you find and run the programs that you need. To explore Program Manager, make sure that its window is active and maximized (see pages 12 and 13).

Cleaning up

When you use the Program Manager window for the first time, it's a good idea to clean up your display, so that you can see where everything is. To do this, hold down the **Shift** key, and press the **F5** key. If any open windows appear inside the Program Manager window, minimize them one by one until your display looks like this:

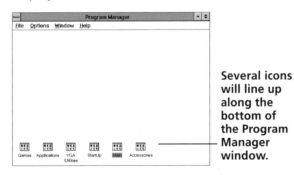

Several icons will line up along the bottom of the Program Manager window.

Program group icons

Program Manager gathers all the programs on your computer into "program groups". Each program group has its own name, and is represented by a "program group icon" inside the Program Manager window.

A program group icon

Each icon is labeled with the name of the group it represents.

Program group windows

To find out which programs a particular program group contains, double-click on its program group icon. A window will appear inside the Program Manager window. This type of window is called a program group window. Once a program group window is open, it displays an icon for each of the programs included in that group.

This screen shows the Accessories program group window open inside Program Manager's window.

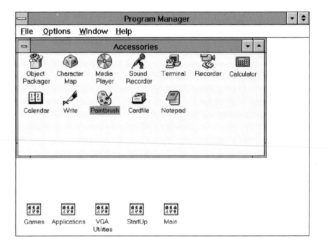

Finding a program

To run a program that you want to use, you need to find the icon that represents that program. To do this, use Program Manager to open and search each program group window until you find the icon you need. You may have to use scroll bars on a program group window to search its contents thoroughly.

Each time you open a program group window, use the **Shift** and **F5** keys to clean up the Program Manager window. If Program Manager becomes cluttered with open program group windows, make some space by minimizing the ones you are not using. This will change them back into program group icons.

Running a program

Once you have found the icon for the program you want, you can start running the program. To do this, you simply double-click on the program's icon.

As a program starts running, its window appears on top of your desktop. The program will remain on your desktop, as a window or an icon, until you stop running it. On page 25 you'll find out how to stop running a program by "closing" its window.

The way out

The Program Manager window also enables you to bring your Windows session to an end. You found out on page 7 how to make Windows stop running by using keystrokes to close the Program Manager window.

Once you've learned how to use clicking to close a window (see page 25) you'll be able to use your mouse, rather than the keyboard, to close Program Manager and quit Windows.

Using menu commands

Like most other windows, the Program Manager window has a menu bar containing several words. When you click on one of the words in a window's menu bar, a list of possible commands called a menu drops down beneath that word. You can select one of these commands by clicking on it.

Some menus include shortcut keystrokes for certain commands. You can use these as an alternative to using your mouse to enter the command.

Choosing commands from menus is one of the main ways in which you use Windows to control your PC.

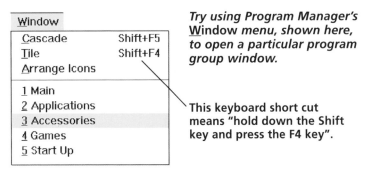

Try using Program Manager's Window menu, shown here, to open a particular program group window.

This keyboard short cut means "hold down the Shift key and press the F4 key".

Disabled menu commands

Some of the commands included in a menu may appear in faded text. These are known as disabled commands. Clicking on a disabled menu command has no effect.

Other parts of the Windows display, such as command buttons, can also appear in disabled form.

This menu includes two disabled commands.

Disabled buttons like these won't respond to clicking.

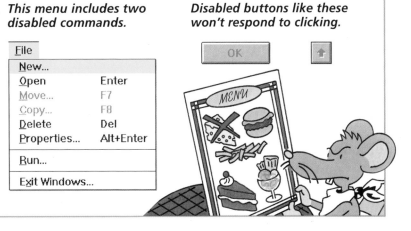

Word processing with Write

Now that you know how to find and run a program, you can try out a Windows application. Use Program Manager to find the icon for a program called Write. It looks like this, and is usually found in the Accessories program group. Double-click on the Write icon to set the Write application running.

What is Write?

Write is an application which enables you to work with text. Text is made up of individual units called characters, which can be letters of the alphabet, numbers, punctuation marks, symbols or even spaces. Write lets you type text into your computer and then organize it to form a document such as a letter or story. This kind of application is called a word processing program.

The Write window

As you start running Write, its window appears on your desktop. This window provides all the tools you will need to create a text document. The area inside the window displays your Write document, which starts off as a blank page. Maximize the Write window to take a closer look at its various parts.

This screen shows the Write window in maximized form. The top left-hand corner is magnified so that you can see it more clearly.

The title bar displays the name of your document ("untitled" at this point).

The menu bar is used to enter your commands (see page 15).

This sign marks where your text ends.

This line is called the insertion point.

Scroll bars enable you to move your view across the document.

This tells you which page of your document you are looking at.

Entering text

The flashing vertical line inside Write's page area is called the insertion point. It shows you where your text will be placed on the page when you start typing. Try it out by typing in the words "Word processing with Write". As you type, the text will appear to the left of the insertion point, as shown below.

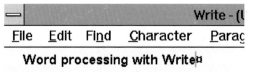

The I-beam

When you point inside Write's page area, the pointer turns into a tall "I" shape. This special pointer is called the I-beam. You use it to position the insertion point anywhere within your document.

Using your mouse, move the I-beam to the left of the word "with". Click the primary mouse button, and the insertion point will jump to this new location. Now type the words "is easy". This new text will insert itself in your document to the left of the insertion point's new position.

Word processing is easy with Write

Deleting text

To erase, or "delete", some of your text, use the I-beam to place the insertion point to the right of the text you want to remove. Press the **Backspace** key to delete one character at a time. The **Backspace** key usually has an arrow on it, pointing to the left. On most keyboards it is found above the **Return** key (see page 6).

Try deleting the words "with Write" that you typed onto your Write page earlier.

The Backspace key

Selecting text

You can also use the I-beam to mark out parts of your document that you want to alter. This is called selecting. To select a section of text, move the I-beam to the left of the first character in that section. Holding down the mouse button, drag the I-beam until it is just to the right of the last character in the section. When you release the mouse button, the selected text remains highlighted, as shown below.

Highlighted Write text looks like this

Deleting a block

You can delete a chunk of text, known as a text "block", by selecting it and pressing the **Backspace** key. All the highlighted text will be removed from your document. Try deleting the remaining words on your Write page in this way.

Shortcut selecting

There are several speedy ways to select parts of your document. To select an individual word, simply double-click the I-beam on it. To select an entire line of text, click in the left-hand margin next to that line with the arrow-shaped pointer, or hold down the **Ctrl** key and click the I-beam somewhere along the line. To select your entire document, hold down the **Ctrl** key and click in the left-hand margin with the arrow-shaped pointer.

WARNING!

While a block of text is selected, any new text that you type in will replace it. To avoid this happening accidentally, you should "deselect" a block of text once you have finished altering it. Click the insertion point somewhere else in your document. The text will be deselected, losing its highlighting.

Writing with Write

You can use what you have learned on these pages to type in a letter to one of your friends. Write will automatically start a new line each time you reach the right-hand margin. If you want to start a new line before you reach the right-hand margin, press the **Return** key. Use the selection and insertion techniques to correct any mistakes you make as you go along.

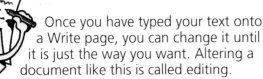

More about Write

Once you have typed your text onto a Write page, you can change it until it is just the way you want. Altering a document like this is called editing.

Choosing a style

Write's _Character_ menu provides a variety of options for editing the appearance of your text. For example, you can choose from several text styles. To do this, select the text that you want to alter, then click on one of the _Character_ menu commands shown in the chart below.

Bold	Makes text thicker
Italic	_Makes text lean to the right_
Underline	<u>Draws a line under text</u>
Regular	Returns text to standard style

When you select a style command, a check mark appears next to it in the _Character_ menu. If you click on a style command with a check mark next to it, the check mark disappears, and the style is switched off. You can combine text styles by picking more than one style command.

√ **Bold**	Ctrl+B	
√ **Italic**	Ctrl+I	
√ **Underline**	Ctrl+U	

See what your text looks like when you combine these three styles.

Sizing your text

The _Character_ menu also lets you alter the size of your text. To do this, first select the text you want to resize. If you want to make this text smaller, click on the _Reduce Font_ command. To make it larger, click on the _Enlarge Font_ command.

The Paragraph menu

As well as altering the style and size of your text, you can choose how you want it to be positioned on your page. The borders that surround the text are called margins. By selecting a block of text, and then clicking on a command in Write's _Paragraph_ menu, you can place the text in different positions between the left and right margins, as shown below.

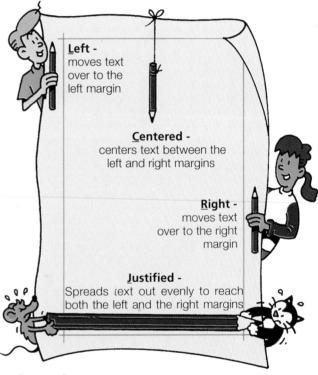

Left - moves text over to the left margin

Centered - centers text between the left and right margins

Right - moves text over to the right margin

Justified - Spreads text out evenly to reach both the left and the right margins

Spacing out your text

You can also use Write's _Paragraph_ menu to choose how much space there is between one line of your text and the next. Select the text block whose line-spacing you want to alter, and choose from the _Single Space_, _1½ Space_, or _Double Space_ commands in the _Paragraph_ menu.

To return text to Write's standard layout (single spaced text, aligned to the left margin), select the text and click on the _Normal_ command in the _Paragraph_ menu.

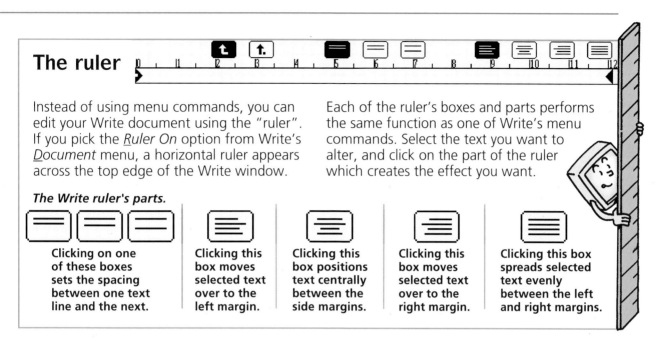

The ruler

Instead of using menu commands, you can edit your Write document using the "ruler". If you pick the *Ruler On* option from Write's *Document* menu, a horizontal ruler appears across the top edge of the Write window.

Each of the ruler's boxes and parts performs the same function as one of Write's menu commands. Select the text you want to alter, and click on the part of the ruler which creates the effect you want.

The Write ruler's parts.

Clicking on one of these boxes sets the spacing between one text line and the next.

Clicking this box moves selected text over to the left margin.

Clicking this box positions text centrally between the side margins.

Clicking this box moves selected text over to the right margin.

Clicking this box spreads selected text evenly between the left and right margins.

Using the Clipboard

You can move a block of text from one place in your document to another using the Windows Clipboard system. Select the text that you want to move. Pick *Cut* from Write's *Edit* menu. The text will be removed from your document and be placed out of sight on the Clipboard. Using the I-beam, move the insertion point to the text's new location. Pick *Paste* from the *Edit* menu and the text will be copied from the Clipboard back into your document.

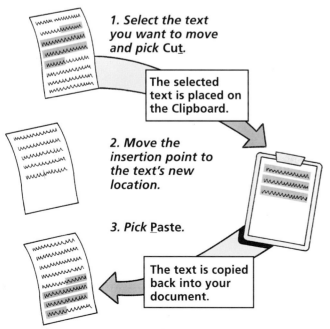

1. Select the text you want to move and pick Cut.

The selected text is placed on the Clipboard.

2. Move the insertion point to the text's new location.

3. Pick Paste.

The text is copied back into your document.

Copying your text

If you select a block of text and pick the *Copy* command from Write's *Edit* menu, the text will be copied onto your Clipboard without being removed from its original location. You can then use the insertion point and the *Paste* command to insert the copied text in other places in your document.

WARNING!
The Clipboard can hold only one chunk of information at a time. Cutting or copying something new onto the Clipboard deletes whatever was previously there.

Clipboard Viewer

If you want to find out what is currently stored on your Clipboard, you can use Program Manager to find and run a program called Clipboard Viewer. This displays the contents of the Clipboard inside a window on your desktop.

The Clipboard Viewer icon

Using dialog boxes

As you use a Windows application, you will come across some menu commands which end in three dots. Whenever you pick one of these commands, Windows displays a questionnaire called a dialog box on your desktop. Dialog boxes let you enter information about what you want to do.

Fonts

An example of a Windows dialog box is the one you use in Write to choose a "font". A font is a complete set of letters, numbers and symbols of a particular appearance. As you create a document, you can choose from a range of fonts, to make your text look just the way you want. Each font has its own name.

This picture shows a selection of the many different text fonts.

ENVISION STAMP GOLDMINE President SCOTT UMBRELLA VIKING MYSTICAL KIDS GALLERIA KEYPUNCH POSSE Frankenstein Merlin

Write's Font box

You can pick a font before you type in your Write text, or select a block of existing text and change it to a particular font. In either case, you use a dialog box to enter your choice of font. Click on the *Fonts...* option in Write's *Character* menu. After a brief pause, Write's Font dialog box will appear on your desktop.

This is Write's Font dialog box.

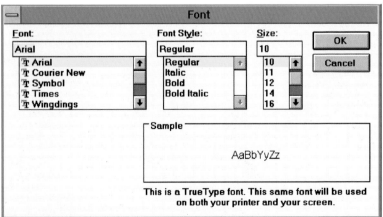

Changing settings

Three smaller boxes inside the Font dialog box display the current text settings. They show the name of the font, and the style and size of the text (see page 18).

By scrolling through the list of possible settings beneath each of these three boxes, and clicking on a font, style and size of your choice, you can enter new text settings.

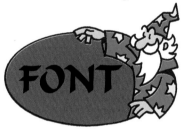

A sample of text in the font, style and size that you have specified appears in the Sample box at the bottom right-hand corner of the Font dialog box. If you are happy with your choices, click the *OK* button. The dialog box will disappear, and your new text settings will take effect.

Dialog controls

Write's Font box is one of the many different dialog boxes you will encounter as you use the Windows system. Some contain special gadgets, such as buttons, boxes or lists. You use each of these gadgets in a particular way to enter information.

This pretend pizza order form gives you an idea of how some of the common dialog box controls work.

This is an OPTION BUTTON. Click on it to select one of several options. A dot appears inside the circle next to the selected option.

You can click on these up and down arrows to make a number setting larger or smaller.

This is a CHECK BOX. Click on it to switch an option on or off. If an option is on, an X appears in its box. You can select more than one check box option.

This is a DROP-DOWN LIST BOX. Click on its arrow button to open a list of options. You can then select one option by clicking on it.

HELP!

To try out the various dialog box gadgets, you can follow the section on dialog boxes in the Windows Tutorial. Find out how to follow a particular section of the Windows Tutorial on page 45.

OK or Cancel?

When you have selected new settings in a dialog box, you make your choices take effect by clicking on the box's *OK* button.

    If you decide that you don't want to make the changes you have selected after all, you can abandon a dialog box by clicking on its *Cancel* button. The dialog box will vanish from the desktop, and your document will remain unchanged.

Writing with Write

Use what you now know about Write's controls and commands to edit the letter that you typed in on page 17. Try aligning your address to the right margin. You could alter the font, style and size of parts of your text, or even use the Clipboard to rearrange the order of your letter.

Whoops!

Write's *Edit* menu includes a command called *Undo*. Whenever you use the ruler, menu commands, the Clipboard or dialog boxes to edit your text, and then regret it, click on *Undo* to cancel your last editing step. Most Windows applications have an *Undo* command.

Saving your work

When you have produced a document using an application, Windows lets you store it away so that you can return to it later. This is known as saving your work.

Disks, drives and files

Inside your computer is a device called a hard disk, which can store lots of information. The hard disk sits inside a hard disk drive, which records information onto it.

Your computer stores each batch of information, such as a Write document, as a "file" on the hard disk. When you want to use a particular piece of information again, the hard disk drive retrieves the file you need.

Floppies

A floppy disk is a small disk, cased in plastic, which can store files in much the same way as a hard disk. You insert a "floppy" into its disk drive through a slot in your computer.

If you save a file on a floppy disk, you can remove the disk from its drive and take the file away to use on another computer.

This cutaway picture of a PC shows the main types of disk drives.

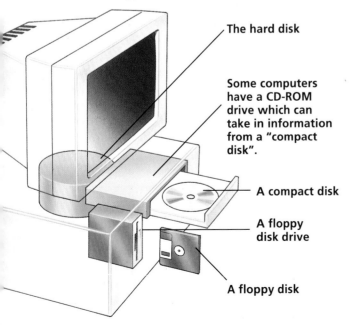

The hard disk

Some computers have a CD-ROM drive which can take in information from a "compact disk".

A compact disk

A floppy disk drive

A floppy disk

The Save As box

Before you can save a document as a file on disk, you need to give it a name, and tell the computer where on disk you want to keep it. Windows applications have a dialog box, called a Save As box, which lets you enter these details when you save a document.

To find out how to use a Save As box, try saving the Write letter that you created on the previous pages. Pick the *Save As...* command from Write's *File* menu. The dialog box below will appear on your desktop:

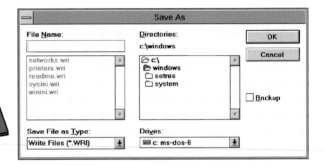

Naming your file

To give your Write letter a name, click the insertion point into the box labeled "File Name" in the top left-hand corner of Write's Save As box. Then type in the name of your choice. You can give a Windows file a name that is up to eight characters long. It cannot include spaces, or any of the characters shown below:

. : / \ [ ] * | < > + = ; , ?

A filename is usually followed by something called an extension. This consists of a period and a three character code. Each application has its own filename extension. Your computer can tell from an extension what type of file it is dealing with. Add the extension ".wri" to your filename to label your file as a Write document.

The File Name box

File **Name**:

maria.wri

You could use your name or initials as a filename.

22

Picking a drive

The next step when saving a file is to choose the disk drive that holds the disk on which you want to store your file.

Near the bottom of the Save As box is a box labeled "Drives". Click on the Drives box to see a drop-down list of all your PC's disk drives.

The Drives box

Dri_v_es:

💻 c: ms-dos-6   ⬇
💻 a:
💻 b:
💻 c: ms-dos-6

Each of your computer's drives is represented in the Drives box by a symbol labeled with a letter.

To save your Write letter on the hard disk, pick the hard disk drive by clicking on it in the Drives list. It is represented by this symbol, and is usually labeled as the "c" drive.

Directories

You can gather the files stored on a disk into groups. This is kind of like organizing lots of paper documents into separate folders. It makes it easier to find a specific file later on. The "folders" on a disk are called directories.

The disk on which you are about to save your file may contain several directories, so you need to specify which one you want to store your file in before you can save it. Above the Drives box in the Save As dialog box is a box labeled "Directories". This displays a list of all the directories on the disk in the drive that you've selected. Each one is represented by a small folder symbol, labeled with a directory name.

Picking a directory

To save your file in a particular directory, you need to find that directory's folder symbol in the Directories list and double-click on it.

You will find out on page 34 how to create a personal directory in which to keep your own work. In the meantime you should save your Write letter in the main directory on the hard disk, known as the hard disk root directory (see page 31). To open this directory, double-click on the folder symbol labeled "c:\" at the top of the Directories list.

The Directories box

Directories:

c:\

📂 c:\   ⬆
📁 dos
📁 mouse
📁 temp
📁 windows ⬇

Giving the OK

You have now told your computer what you want to call your file and where you want to store it. Click on the Save As box's *OK* button, and your computer will save your document. The Save As dialog box will disappear, and your document's filename will appear across the title bar of the Write window. A copy of your letter is now safely stored as a file in the root directory on the hard disk.

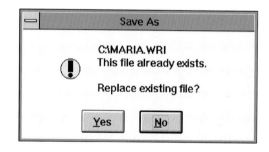

HELP!

This box may appear on your screen when you try to save your document. This means that the directory you've picked already contains a file with the name that you've chosen. Click the _N_o button, use the Save As box to give your file a different name, and try the *OK* button again.

Save As
C:\MARIA.WRI
This file already exists.

Replace existing file?

[Yes]   [_N_o] |

More about files

On these pages, you will find out how to retrieve a Windows file from disk when you want to use it. You will also learn how to keep your files up to date.

The Open box

Retrieving a file from disk is known as opening a file. To enable you to find and open any file previously created using an application, Windows provides a special dialog box, called an Open box.

Try opening the file that you saved on page 23. Make sure that Write's window is open and active. If it still contains your letter, pick the *New* command from the *File* menu to clear away this document, so that you can try retrieving it from disk. Click on the *Open...* command in the Write window's *File* menu. Write's Open box will appear on your desktop.

Write's Open box.

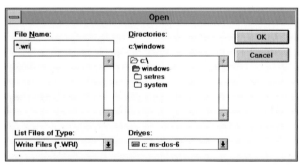

Opening a directory

You use an Open box to tell your computer the name of the file you want to open, and where to find it. Your Write letter file is

stored in the root directory on your PC's hard disk (see page 23). Use the "Drives" list inside Write's Open box to pick the hard disk drive. Then use the "Directories" list to open up the root directory, just as you did on page 23.

Selecting a file

Once you have opened a directory, a list of filenames appears in the left-hand part of the Open box. This is an alphabetical list of all the files in the open directory that match the application you are using. Because you are using Write's Open box, the list will show all the files in the directory that end in ".wri".

Scroll through the list of filenames until you find the one you want. By clicking on your letter's filename, you can enter it into the "File Name" box at the top of the list.

Now that you've told your computer which file you want to open, and where to find it, click on the *OK* button. Your PC will retrieve the file from disk. The Open box will vanish, and your letter will appear in the Write window.

The File Name box

File **Name**:

| maria.wri |

| maria.wri |

The **S**ave option

If you alter a document after you've retrieved it from disk, you may want to save the new version.

There is no need to use the Save As box, as you did on page 22, to save the new version of your document. Your file already has a name and disk location. Instead you can simply click on the *Save* command in the *File* menu. Your computer will automatically store the latest version of your document in its original disk location, under its original filename.

Keeping up to date

As you work on a Windows document, you should use the *Save* command regularly to keep the version on disk "updated". This means that if your PC's power supply fails for any reason, you will be able to retrieve the most recent version of your document from disk.

Closing a window

To make a Windows program stop running, you have to close its window. To do this you click on the control-menu box in the top left-hand corner of the window (see page 8). The window's "control menu" will appear. Pick the *Close* command from this control menu. As a speedy alternative, you can close a window simply by double-clicking on its control-menu box.

When you have finished your Write letter, and saved the latest version of it on disk, close the Write window.

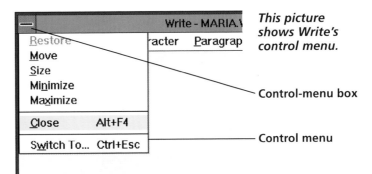

This picture shows Write's control menu.

Control-menu box

Control menu

Saving current changes

When you try to close a window, a box may appear on your screen telling you that you have changed your document since the last time you saved it. Your computer is checking whether or not you want to save the latest document version before you close its window.

If you want to save the current version of your document over the previous version, click the *Yes* button. If you don't want to save the current version, click *No*.

If you want to keep both the previous and current versions, click the *Cancel* button to return to your document, and use the *Save As...* command to save the current version under a new filename.

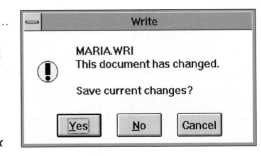

Write's "Save changes?" box

Paintbrush

This is the icon for Paintbrush, a Windows application which lets you create pictures on your screen. Use Program Manager to find and run the Paintbrush program. When the Paintbrush window appears on your desktop, maximize it so that you can take a closer look.

Picking a canvas size

The main area of the Paintbrush window shows a canvas on which you can create a picture. You can specify the size of the canvas you want to use, and choose whether you want your picture to be in color or black and white. To do this, pick *Image Attributes...* from the *Options* menu. The dialog box shown below will appear:

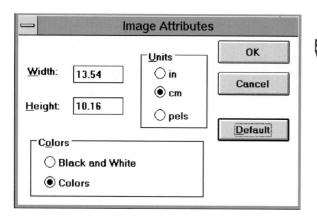

To set your canvas to a standard size, click on the *Default* button. If you want to paint with a variety of colors, make sure that the *Colors* option is selected. Then click the *OK* button.

Your canvas will now be slightly larger than the Paintbrush window's picture display area, so Paintbrush provides scroll bars to enable you to move your view across your canvas.

Choosing colors

Paintbrush provides several different drawing tools and a range of colored paints to use them with.

To choose colors for your picture, you use the multicolored strip at the bottom of the Paintbrush window. This is called the Palette.

Part of the Palette

You can pick both a foreground color to draw with, and a background color to draw on. You will find out how each Paintbrush tool uses these two colors on the opposite page.

To pick a foreground color, click on a color in the Palette with the primary mouse button. To pick a background color, click on a Palette color with the secondary mouse button (see page 10). The box at the left-hand end of the Palette shows the colors you have chosen:

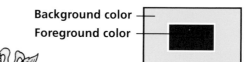

The Toolbox

At the left-hand edge of the Paintbrush window is a panel of eighteen small pictures, called the Toolbox. You use the Toolbox to choose from Paintbrush's drawing tools, each of which creates a different effect on your canvas.

To select a tool, click on it in the Toolbox so that it is highlighted. You can then move it around the canvas using your mouse. Most tools appear in the picture area as a cross-shaped pointer, but some have their own particular pointer shape.

This is the Toolbox panel.

Special effects

The picture below shows some of the effects you can create using different drawing tools and colors. Try producing your own Paintbrush work of art!

 You can use the Brush tool like a crayon, dragging it to make a mark on the canvas in the foreground color.

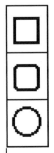 These tools let you drag out different shaped outlines. By holding down the Shift key as you use a tool, you can use the Ellipse tool to draw a perfect circle, or the Box tool to draw a perfect square. The outlines appear in the current foreground color.

 The Airbrush tool sprays the foreground color onto the canvas as you drag it around.

 Dragging the Eraser tool over part of your picture erases it by coloring over it in the background color.

 As you drag the Color Eraser across the canvas, it replaces any areas of the foreground color with the background color.

 Clicking the Paint Roller tool inside an enclosed area fills in that area with the foreground color.

The Polygon tool lets you drag out a series of connected lines to create a many-sided shape called a polygon. The free end of the last line must join up with the free end of the first line to form a closed shape.

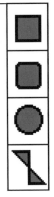 These tools let you drag out a filled-in shape. The border appears in the background color, and the shape is filled in with the foreground color.

The Line tool lets you draw a straight line. Drag the cross-shaped pointer from where you want the line to start, to where you want it to end. If you hold down the Shift key as you drag the Line tool you can draw vertical, horizontal and 45° diagonal lines.

This tool lets you drag out a straight line and then bend it twice, by dragging, to create a curve.

Changing your brush

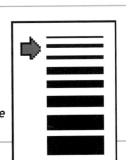

You can change the width of the Brush, Eraser, Color Eraser and Airbrush tools. Click on the width you want in the Linesize box in the bottom left-hand corner of the Paintbrush window. You can also use the Linesize box to set the thickness of curves, straight lines and the outlines of shapes.

The Linesize box

More about Paintbrush

Once you have drawn a Paintbrush picture, you can add text to it, or zoom in on part of it to add details. You can even cut pieces out so that you can move or alter them.

Adding text

To add text to your picture, select the Text tool from the Toolbox.

As you move the pointer across the picture area, it will turn into an I-beam, like the one you used in Write. Position this I-beam where you want to add text to your picture, and click. An insertion point will appear, enabling you to type text onto your canvas in the current foreground color.

The Text tool **abc**

Paintbrush styles

Like Write, Paintbrush lets you vary the appearance of text. You can use Paintbrush's *Text* menu to select a font and text size, or to pick the bold, italic or underline styles. Paintbrush also has two extra text style options. The *Outline* command produces foreground colored text with a thin outline in the background color. *Shadow* produces foreground colored text with a shadow in the background color.

The Outline style   *The Shadow style*

Changing your view

A standard Paintbrush window displays the Palette, the Toolbox, the Linesize box, and part of your canvas. But you can alter this standard view if you want.

If you pick *Zoom Out* from the *View* menu, Paintbrush displays your picture at a smaller scale, so that the entire canvas fits inside the picture area. You will find out on the opposite page why you may sometimes need to use this zoom out view. To return to the standard view, select *Zoom In* from the *View* menu.

To take a look at your picture without the Paintbrush controls around it, select the *View Picture* command from the *View* menu. To return to the controls, click anywhere on the display.

A Paintbrush window showing the standard view.   *A Paintbrush window showing the Zoom Out view.*

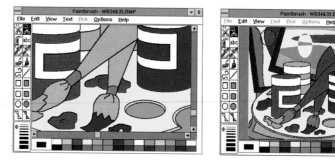

Zooming in close

You can work in detail on a small section of your picture by picking *Zoom In* from the *View* menu. Your pointer will change into a small rectangular box. Use your mouse to move this box over the section of your picture that you want to look at in detail, then click. The picture area will display a close-up of the selected section, showing the tiny squares, called pixels, which make up your picture.

You can alter the picture section one pixel at a time. Click the foreground color into a pixel using the primary mouse button, or the background color using the secondary mouse button.

When you have finished adding details to your picture section, select *Zoom Out* from the *View* menu to return to the standard Paintbrush view.

The Zoom In view

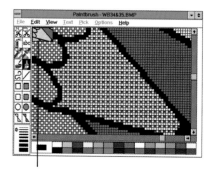

This box shows the picture section at actual size.

The cutout tools

The Toolbox includes two "cutout" tools. You use these to outline a section of your picture so that you can move it to a new position on your canvas, or alter it using the commands in Paintbrush's _Pick_ menu.

These are the two cutout tools.

The **Scissor** tool lets you draw a wavy outline to create an irregularly shaped cutout section.

The **Pick** tool lets you drag out a rectangular outline to create a box-shaped cutout section.

Moving part of picture

Once you have cut out a section of your picture, you can drag it to a new position on your canvas. When the section is where you want it, click somewhere outside its outline and Paintbrush will place the section back on the canvas.

Alternatively, you can choose the _Cut_ or _Copy_ command from the _Edit_ menu to place a cutout section on the Windows Clipboard. Pick _Paste_, and a copy of the cutout will appear in the top left-hand corner of the picture area. You can then drag the cutout section wherever you want on the canvas and click it into place.

WARNING!

When you click a cutout picture section into place, any part that doesn't fit within the picture display area is trimmed off. If you want to avoid this happening, select _Zoom Out_ before you use a cutout tool. You can then use the Pick tool and the _Cut_, _Copy_ and _Paste_ commands to move cutout sections without damaging them.

Using the Pick menu

You can use the commands in Paintbrush's _Pick_ menu to alter the appearance of parts of your picture. Use one of the cutout tools to outline the section you want to alter, then click on a _Pick_ menu command.

This diagram shows what the Pick commands do.

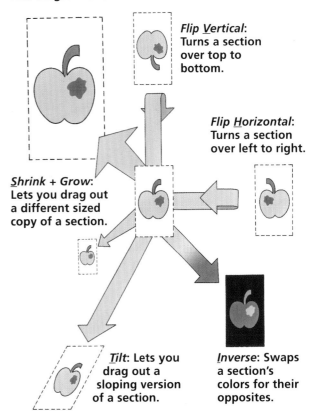

Flip Vertical: Turns a section over top to bottom.

Flip Horizontal: Turns a section over left to right.

Shrink + Grow: Lets you drag out a different sized copy of a section.

Tilt: Lets you drag out a sloping version of a section.

Inverse: Swaps a section's colors for their opposites.

Saving your artworks

You can keep a Paintbrush picture on disk just like any other Windows document. Use _Save As..._ to store your picture in the root directory on the hard disk (see pages 22 and 23). Because you are saving a Paintbrush file, you need to use the Paintbrush filename extension, which is ".bmp". When you have completed and saved your picture, close Paintbrush's window.

Using File Manager

As you save more and more files on disk, it's important to keep track of where each one is stored. Windows has a program, called File Manager, which helps you do this.

Use Program Manager to find and run the File Manager program. It is usually found in a program group called Main. When the File Manager window opens on your desktop, maximize it to take a closer look.

This is File Manager's icon.

Avoiding accidents

File Manager lets you move files from one place to another on disk, change their filenames, or even delete them completely. You need to be careful not to do any of these things by accident.

File Manager has a safety system to prevent accidental alterations. As soon as you open its window, check that this safety system is switched on. To do this, pick the *Confirmation...* command from the *Options* menu. Make sure that the dialog box which appears is filled in like the one below, with an X in each of its five check boxes. Then click the *OK* button. File Manager will now ask for confirmation whenever you try to move, delete or alter a file.

File Manager's Confirmation box

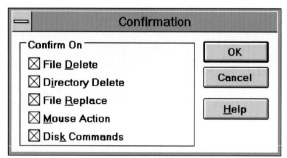

A neat display

To help you find your way around File Manager for the first time, it's a good idea to convert its window to a standard layout.

Hold down **Shift** and press the **F5** key. One or more windows will appear in a stack inside the File Manager window. These are called directory windows.

As a beginner, it's best to have only one directory window open at a time. So close all but one of the directory windows, using their control-menu boxes (see page 25).

Pick *Tree and Directory* from File Manager's *View* menu. This will divide the remaining directory window into two equal areas.

Your File Manager window will now look like this.

A directory window

Using a directory window

Files are grouped into separate directories on disk (see page 23). A File Manager directory window enables you to look inside a directory to see what files it holds.

It's possible to have several directory windows open inside File Manager, but only one of these windows can be active at a time. You can find out on the opposite page what the various parts of a directory window are used for.

The disk drive bar

Instead of a menu bar, a directory window has a bar containing several small symbols. Each symbol represents one of your computer's disk drives.

When you want to look at the contents of a particular disk, you select the drive which contains that disk by clicking on its symbol. Try clicking on the hard disk drive symbol (see page 23) to find out what files are stored on your hard disk.

A directory window disk drive bar

As you select the hard drive's symbol, it will be outlined by a box.

The name of the disk in the selected drive appears at the right-hand end of the bar.

The directory tree

The left-hand side of a directory window shows a diagram, called a directory tree. This represents the arrangement of directories on the disk inside the selected disk drive. Files grouped together in a directory are often separated again into further directories. The directories within a particular directory are known as its subdirectories. The directory tree diagram shows this arrangement as a series of folders inside other folders.

To take a closer look at the tree layout, select *Expand All* from File Manager's *Tree* menu, and use the scroll bar at the right-hand side of the directory tree to move your view to the top of the tree.

Roots and branches

Every disk has one main directory, called the root directory, which contains all the other directories on that disk. The root directory on the selected disk is represented by a folder symbol at the very top of the directory tree. Lines called branches run from the root directory symbol to other folder symbols, each representing a subdirectory inside the root directory. Some of these folders also have branches running to other folders, showing how they in turn are divided into subdirectories.

A directory tree

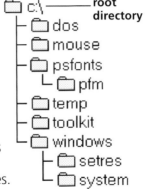

Directory contents

You will find out on page 32 how to use the directory tree to find and select the directory that you want to look inside. Once a directory is selected in the tree, the right-hand side of the directory window shows a list of its contents.

A directory contents list

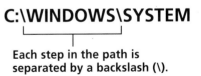

Paths

A directory window's title bar shows the "path" for the directory currently selected in the tree. This describes the route to the directory along the branches of the directory tree.

For example, if you wanted to look in the "system" directory inside the "windows" directory on the hard disk, you would need to open the hard disk root directory (labeled "c:"), open the "windows" directory inside that, and open the "system" directory inside that. The path for this directory would be written like this:

C:\WINDOWS\SYSTEM

Each step in the path is separated by a backslash (\).

Finding your files

Whenever you want to retrieve one of your Windows documents from disk, you can use File Manager to find and open its file.

Which disk?

To find a file, you first have to tell your computer which disk it is stored on. To do this, use the active directory window's disk drive bar, as described on page 31, to select the drive that holds the disk you want.

Picking a directory

Once you have selected a drive, the active directory window will display a directory tree for the disk inside it. Search this directory tree to find the directory in which your file is stored.

Sometimes the directory tree doesn't show the subdirectories contained within certain directories. You might have to alter the tree's layout so that it includes a separate folder symbol for the subdirectory that contains your file. This is known as expanding the directory tree.

Expanding branches

To expand the directory tree so that it shows a specific directory's subdirectories, select that directory by clicking on its folder symbol, and pick *Expand Branch* from File Manager's *Tree* menu. Alternatively, you can simply double-click on the directory's folder symbol. The directory's subdirectories will appear in the tree diagram.

The Windows directory before and after it is expanded

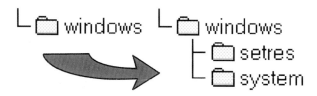

Expanding tips

To help you remember which directories contain subdirectories, make sure there is a check next to *Indicate Expandable Branches* in File Manager's *Tree* menu. A small "+" sign will appear inside the folder symbol of any directory that contains subdirectories which are not shown in the tree.

The easiest way to ensure that the directory tree displays the entire layout of directories and subdirectories, showing a separate folder symbol for each one, is to pick *Expand All* from File Manager's *Tree* menu.

The contents list

When you have found the directory containing your file, click on its folder symbol to open it up. A list of the directory's contents will appear in the right-hand half of the directory window.

The directory contents list

Each of your document files is represented by this symbol

🗀 setres		09/07/9
🗀 system		01/07/9
🗎 thatch.bmp	598	10/03/9
🗎 zigzag.bmp	630	30/11/9
🗎 cal.cal	192	29/03/9
🖳 mouse.com	56408	10/03/9
🖳 win.com	44170	06/12/9
🗋 panose.dat	135483	05/05/9
🗋 reg.dat	16657	01/02/9
🗋 wintutor.dat	57356	10/03/9
🗋 aldlearn.dll	29184	14/06/9

Opening a file

Use the scroll bar at the right-hand edge of the directory window to look through the directory contents list. When you find the file you want, open it by clicking on its filename so that it is highlighted, and picking the *Open* command from File Manager's *File* menu. Alternatively, you can simply double-click on its filename.

As you open the file, the window of the application that you used to create it will appear on your desktop, containing your document.

Finding lost files

The instructions on the opposite page only enable you to find and open a file if you can remember where it is stored. If you've forgotten where the file you want is kept, you'll need to use File Manager's *Search...* command to track it down.

The Search box

To find a lost file, you first have to tell your computer which part of which disk you want it to search. If you can remember which directory the file you want is in, use File Manager's active directory window to find and select it. If you can't remember, select the root directory so that your computer will search the entire disk.

Once you have selected a directory, pick *Search...* from File Manager's *File* menu. The Search dialog box will appear on your desktop.

File Manager's Search dialog box

Search	
Search For:	*.*
Start From:	C:\
☒ Search All Subdirectories	
	OK
	Cancel
	Help

Specifying a search range

The "Start From" box inside the Search dialog box shows the path for the directory you are about to search (see page 31). If you decide that you want your computer to search a different directory from the one currently selected in the tree, type the alternative directory's path in the Start From box.

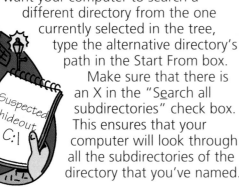

Make sure that there is an X in the "Search all subdirectories" check box. This ensures that your computer will look through all the subdirectories of the directory that you've named.

Entering a search name

The "Search For" box inside the Search dialog box lets you type in the name of the file that you're looking for. If you can't remember the exact filename, you can enter an approximate version. Substitute a "*" character in the place of any part of the name that you've forgotten. Your computer will try to find a filename which matches your approximation.

Search results

Once you have entered a search range and name, click the *OK* button to start your search. File Manager will track down all the files inside the search range with filenames that match your Search For name.

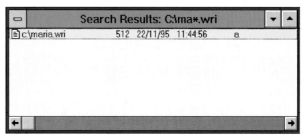

A window will appear inside the File Manager window, listing the names of any files which match your search details. If you can see the file you are looking for in the Results window, you can open it up by selecting it and picking *Open* from the *File* menu, or by double-clicking on its name.

The Search Results window

Search Results: C:\ma*.wri			
≣ c:\maria.wri	512	22/11/95 11:44:56	a

Organizing your files

If you want to rearrange your files on disk, you can use File Manager to move them around. These pages tell you how to use the active directory window to organize your files.

Your own directory

The best way of organizing your files so that they are easy to find is to create a directory of your own to keep them in. Try creating a personal directory on your computer's hard disk. Select the hard disk root directory in the directory tree, and pick *Create Directory...* from File Manager's *File* menu. A dialog box will appear, enabling you to type in a name for your new directory. As with filenames, directory names can only have eight characters, and cannot include spaces, or any of the characters shown below:

. : / \ [ ] * | < > + = ; , ?

When you have entered a directory name, click the *OK* button. Your new personal directory will appear in the tree, as a subdirectory of the hard disk root directory. You can store all your future files inside this directory by selecting it whenever you use a Save As box (see pages 22 and 23).

Source to destination

You can use File Manager to move a file from one directory to another on a disk. To do this, use the active directory window to take the file from its original disk location, known as its source, and put it in a new location, known as its destination. The diagram below shows how you use the active directory window to move a file.

Moving a file

1. Make sure the destination directory is displayed in the directory tree. Expand the tree if necessary.

2. Open the source directory and find the file that you want to move in the directory contents list.

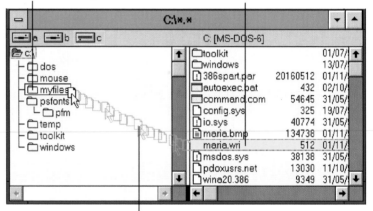

3. Drag the file across onto the folder symbol of the destination directory. As you drag a file it appears as a small document symbol.

4. When the document symbol is correctly positioned over the destination directory, the directory is outlined by a box. Release the mouse button.

Try moving the Write letter file that you saved on page 23, and the Paintbrush picture file that you saved on page 29, into your own directory on your computer's hard disk.

Copying a file

You can create a copy of a file and put it in another directory without removing the original from its source directory. To do this, follow the same procedure as for moving a file, but hold down the **Ctrl** key as you drag the file into the destination directory. This will leave a copy of the file in both the source and destination directories.

Disk to disk

File Manager even lets you transfer a file from one disk to another. This is useful if you want to copy a file from your hard disk onto a floppy disk, so that you can move it to another PC.

To copy a file from one disk to another, you first have to open up the directory you want to copy the file into. Use File Manager's active directory window to open this directory on the destination disk.

Next use the directory window to look for the file that you want to copy on the source disk. When you find the file, drag it onto the disk drive bar. Position it over the symbol of the drive which contains the destination disk, and release the mouse button.

Copying a file to a different disk

When the file is positioned correctly, a black box will outline the destination drive's symbol.

To move a file from one disk to another, rather than copy it, hold down the **Shift** key as you drag the file onto the destination drive's symbol.

Using Re<u>n</u>ame

If you decide that you want to change the name of a file or directory, use the active directory window to find and select it. Then pick *Re<u>n</u>ame...* from File Manager's *<u>F</u>ile* menu. Use the dialog box that appears on your desktop to enter a new name, and click *OK*.

Deleting files

If you want to get rid of a file completely, use the active directory window to find and select it. Then pick *<u>D</u>elete* from the *<u>F</u>ile* menu.

Multiple selection

File Manager lets you handle several files at once. To do this, you need to select the files from the directory contents list, using the multiple selection technique shown below.

Selecting multiple files

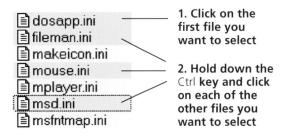

dosapp.ini — **1. Click on the first file you want to select**
fileman.ini
makeicon.ini
mouse.ini — **2. Hold down the Ctrl key and click on each of the other files you want to select**
mplayer.ini
msd.ini
msfntmap.ini

Once you have selected them, you can move, copy or delete multiple files using the same techniques as you would for an individual file.

WARNING!

Each time you move, copy or delete files, a box will appear on your desktop asking you to confirm your command. Always check the details in this box before you give File Manager the go-ahead by clicking *<u>Y</u>es*.

A typical File Manager confirmation box

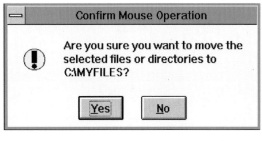

Confirm Mouse Operation

Are you sure you want to move the selected files or directories to C:\MYFILES?

Yes   No

Never delete, move, or rename any files other than your own. They may be essential to your computer's proper functioning, or important to another user.

Printing a document

Once you have created a Windows document, you can use a printer to produce a copy of it on paper.

On and On-line

Before you try to print a document, make sure that your printer is plugged in, connected to your computer, and switched on. You also need to check that the printer is "on-line", which means that it is ready to receive information from your PC. Usually you press an on-line button on the printer. A light comes on to show you that the printer is on-line.

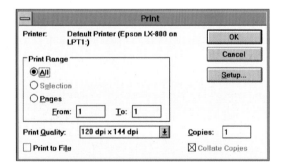

The Print box

Windows applications have a Print dialog box, which lets you give your PC the information it needs to print your document properly.

Try printing out the letter that you created on pages 16 to 21. Open the Write window and open your letter file. Select the *Print...* command from Write's *File* menu. Write's Print box, shown below, will appear:

Print
Printer: Default Printer (Epson LX-800 on LPT1:)

Print Range
- ◉ All
- ○ Selection
- ○ Pages
  - From: 1   To: 1

Print Quality: 120 dpi x 144 dpi ▼   Copies: 1
☐ Print to File   ☒ Collate Copies

[OK] [Cancel] [Setup...]

How many copies?

The *Copies* setting inside a Print box lets you tell your computer how many copies of your document you want. To print a single copy of your letter, type "1" in the *Copies* setting box.

Which pages?

If your document has several pages, the *Print Range* setting lets you specify which of these pages you want to print. To print your entire letter, select *All* in the *Print Range* setting box.

You are now ready to start printing. Click the *OK* button. The Print dialog box will vanish and a smaller box will appear on your desktop, confirming that your document is being printed.

Printing problems

Your computer may be set up so that Windows automatically runs a special program called Print Manager whenever you print a document. If anything goes wrong with the printout, Print Manager displays a message on your desktop, advising you what to do to overcome the printing problem.

If you have difficulties printing your document, and Print Manager fails to help, run through the following check list:

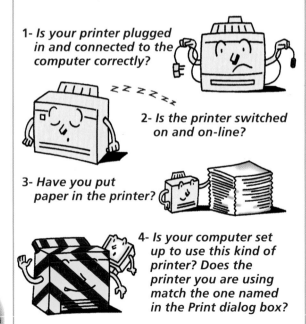

1- Is your printer plugged in and connected to the computer correctly?

2- Is the printer switched on and on-line?

3- Have you put paper in the printer?

4- Is your computer set up to use this kind of printer? Does the printer you are using match the one named in the Print dialog box?

Exploring applications

By working with Write and Paintbrush, you have come across the main parts of the Windows system and used all the standard Windows techniques. You can now use what you have learned to explore other Windows applications on your computer.

Finding your way around

Approach unfamiliar applications step-by-step, using the techniques described in this book. If you need a reminder of how to perform a particular task, flick to the relevant page to refresh your memory. You could start your explorations by trying out the Windows application called Notepad.

This noticeboard shows how you can apply what you know to approach Notepad for the first time.

HELP!
As you explore a new application, make use of the instructions included in the Windows Help system. You can find out how to use these Help instructions on pages 44 and 45.

① Find and run the Notepad program using Program Manager.
Pages 14&15

④ If you want a copy of your Notepad notes on paper, use a printer to print them out.
Page 36

② Use the Notepad window on your desktop to create a text document.
Pages 16&17

⑤ When you have finished with Notepad, save your notes as a file on disk, and close the Notepad window.
Pages 22-25

③ Edit your document using menu commands and dialog boxes.
Pages 18-21

⑥ Use File Manager if you want to move, copy, or rename your Notepad files.
Pages 30-35

Not quite Write

Some applications will seem very different from the ones you've used so far. They won't look much like Write or Paintbrush, and might be used for other things than creating documents. But you can still use your mouse skills to control these applications on your desktop, and your experience of menus and dialog boxes to explore what they can do.

For an example of a very different kind of Windows application, try out a program called Solitaire, included in the Games program group. Solitaire's window lets you play a solo card game on your Windows desktop.

The Solitaire window

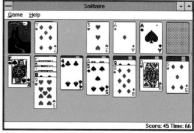

Windows gadgets

These pages introduce some of the other handy applications included in the standard Windows software.

Use the approach described on the previous page to explore each of these applications. They are usually found in a program group called Accessories.

Calculator

 The Windows Calculator is useful if you have any math to do. You operate it just like an ordinary calculator, using the pointer to click on its buttons.

Calculator looks like this.

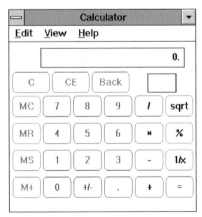

If you pick the *Scientific* command from the *View* menu, lots of extra buttons appear. You can use these if you need to carry out more complicated calculations.

Notepad

 Notepad enables you to jot down lists, reminders, or other straightforward text documents. You type your text onto a page within a window, using an I-beam and insertion point system just like Write's. Unlike Write, however, Notepad has only one font, and few editing options.

By choosing *Word Wrap* from Notepad's *Edit* menu, you can make sure that your text always fits within the window's side borders, as it does in the picture below.

This is a Notepad window.

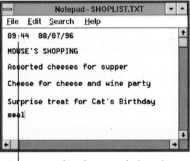

To stamp the date and time in your notes, press the F5 key.

If you want to save your notes as a file on disk, remember to use the Notepad filename extension, ".txt". To print out your shopping list or memo, pick *Print* from Notepad's *File* menu.

Clock

 The Clock application displays a clock-face inside a window on your desktop. You can make this clock-face as large or small as you like by changing the size of Clock's window. The *Settings* menu lets you choose between a clock-face with hands (analog) or with numbers (digital).

The analog clock-face

The digital clock-face

To pick a font for the digital clock-face, use the *Set Font...* command in Clock's *Settings* menu. If you want to hide the Clock window's title and menu bars, pick *No Title* from the *Settings* menu. To display them again, double-click anywhere on the clock-face.

You can choose to have the Clock window permanently on top of your desktop. To do this, pick *Always on Top* from Clock's control menu.

Calendar

 This application lets you create your own Windows calendar. When you first open the Calendar window, it shows a blank page listing the hours of the day. To add a reminder or appointment, simply type it onto this blank schedule. You can use arrow buttons beneath Calendar's menu bar to flick through similar schedules for other dates.

Calendar's daily view

If you press the **F9** key, Calendar will display a monthly calendar. Use the arrow buttons to flick backward or forward through the months of the year. You can mark a particular date for special attention by clicking on it and then picking the *Mark...* command from the *Options* menu. If you double-click on a date, Calendar displays the schedule for that day.

Calendar's monthly view

You can create separate calendars for your home, school or work schedule, for birthdays, or for other important events. Save each calendar as a separate file on disk using the filename extension ".cal".

Cardfile

 Cardfile lets you store information on an alphabetically ordered set of cards. It is ideal for noting down addresses, telephone numbers, or similar details.

To add a new card to a cardfile, press **F7**. A dialog box will appear asking you to enter an "index line" for the new card. This is the title by which the card will be alphabetically sorted. For instance, if you were creating a cardfile of friends' addresses, each card would have a friend's name as an index line.

Once you have typed in an index line for your new card, it will be slotted into its alphabetical position in your cardfile. You can then type whatever information you like onto the card.

This Cardfile window shows a sample address file.

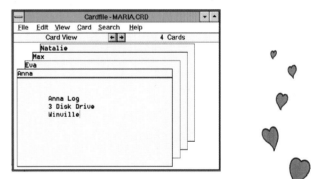

You can create as many cardfiles as you like. Save each one as a separate file on disk, using the filename extension ".crd". When you want to look at the information stored in one of your cardfiles, use the *Open...* command in Cardfile's *File* menu to retrieve it from disk.

To find a particular card, use the arrow buttons beneath the window's menu bar to flick through your cardfile. Alternatively, you can use the *Go To...* command in Cardfile's *Search* menu to specify the index line of the card that you want to look at. Cardfile will then retrieve the card automatically.

The *Print* command in Cardfile's *File* menu lets you print out one or all of the cards in a cardfile, so that you can have a copy of the stored information on paper.

Organizing your desktop

Windows lets you have several programs on your desktop at the same time. These pages tell you how to organize your desktop as it becomes crowded with windows and icons.

Switching

There are all kinds of occasions when you need to run several programs. For example, if you were writing a story using Write, you might want to open a Paintbrush window to create illustrations for your story. You might also want to look in your Windows Notepad (see page 38) to find plot ideas that you jotted down earlier.

This screen shows a busy desktop.

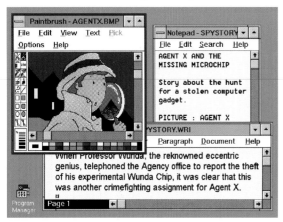

As your desktop becomes crowded with windows and icons, it gets harder to find the program that you want to use next. You need to bring that program's window to the top of the desktop. This is known as switching.

Usually you can switch to a program by clicking on part of its window or, if it is running in minimized form, by double-clicking on its icon. But if you can't see either the program's window or its icon, you'll need to use one of the following special switching techniques.

Using Alt+Tab

The first way of switching to a program which is running, but which you can't find on your desktop, is to use the **Alt** and **Tab** keys. Hold down the **Alt** key and press the **Tab** key. A box will appear in the middle of your screen showing the icon and name of a running program.

The Alt+Tab switching box

Keep **Alt** held down and press **Tab** repeatedly. Each of the programs that are running will appear in the box in turn. When the icon and name of the program you want appear, release the **Alt** key, and the selected program's window will jump to the top of the desktop.

The Task List

The second way of switching to a hidden program is to use a box known as the Task List. Hold down the **Ctrl** key and press the **Esc** key. Release both keys and the Task List box will appear on your desktop.

The Task List box

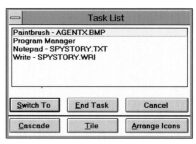

The Task List shows a list of all the programs currently running on your desktop. You can look through this list and highlight the program that you want to use by clicking on its name. Click on the Task List's *Switch To* button to bring this program's window to the top of your desktop.

Cascade and Tile

The Task List box contains several other useful buttons. Clicking the Cascade button gathers all the windows that are currently open into a tidy pile in the middle of your desktop. The active window lies on top of the pile. Clicking the Tile button changes the size of all open windows so that they fit neatly next to one another on your desktop.

Using either Cascade or Tile creates a space at the bottom of the display for the icons of any programs that are running in minimized form. If these icons become scattered around your desktop, you can line them up neatly by clicking the Arrange Icons button in the Task List box.

Cascaded windows

Tiled windows

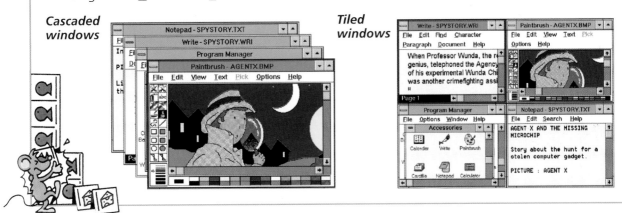

Clearing up

The more programs you have running, the slower your computer will work. So it's a good idea to close programs that you have finished with.

You can find out on page 25 how to close a window using its control-menu box. To close a program which is running in minimized form, click on its icon. The program's control menu will appear. Click on Close. The program will stop running and vanish from the desktop.

You can also use the Task List to clear away programs. Call up the Task List, select the name of the program that you want to close, and click on the End Task button.

The ideal layout

Controlling several programs is easiest if you have only one program's window open at a time. All the other programs should be running in minimized form, lined up as icons along the bottom edge of the desktop.

To set up this layout, minimize all but one of the windows on your desktop. Then call up the Task List and click on its Tile button. This desktop layout gives you plenty of room in the window you are using. It also lets you switch quickly to other running programs when you need to.

To switch from one program to another, simply minimize the window on screen and double-click on the icon of the program you want to use next. Then use the Tile button to make the new active window a convenient size.

This screen shows the ideal desktop layout.

Combining applications

Windows lets you move information from one document to another. You can even combine information created by different applications. As an example of this, these pages show you how to combine Paintbrush and Write to produce an illustrated text document.

Moving a picture

Once you've inserted a picture in your Write letter, you can change its position so that your combined document looks just the way you want it to.

Transferring information with Clipboard

The simplest way to combine Windows applications is to use the Clipboard, introduced on page 19, to transfer information between them.

Try inserting a Paintbrush picture in the Write document that you produced on pages 16 to 21. To do this, first use Paintbrush to produce an illustration for your letter. When you've finished your drawing, use the Pick or Scissor tool to cut it out (see page 29). Copy this cutout onto the Clipboard by picking *Copy* from Paintbrush's *Edit* menu. Then save your picture, as described on pages 22 and 23, and close Paintbrush's window.

The Clipboard now holds a copy of your Paintbrush picture. To insert it in your letter, open your Write file (see page 24). Position the insertion point where you want the illustration to appear in your letter. Pick *Paste* from Write's *Edit* menu. Your Paintbrush picture will be copied from the Clipboard into your document.

Pictures and text cannot appear on the same line in a Write document. The text of your letter will split so that it fits above and below the inserted Paintbrush picture.

This diagram shows how you can use Clipboard to move information from one application to another.

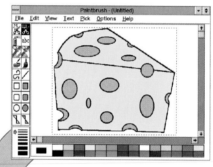

1. Select the information you want to move, and use the Copy command to place it on the Clipboard.

2. Open the document in which you want to insert the information, and use Paste to copy it off the Clipboard.

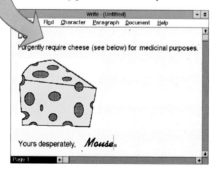

To move your picture to the left or right in your document, first select it by clicking on it with the I-beam. Then pick the *Move Picture* command from Write's *Edit* menu. A square pointer will appear near the middle of the inserted picture.

Write's special square pointer

By moving the square pointer with your mouse, you can shift your picture's outline across your document. Position the outline where you want the picture to be. Then click, and the picture will be moved to this new location.

To move your picture to a completely different place in your Write document, select it with the I-beam, and place it back on the Clipboard using the *Cut* command. You can then use the insertion point and *Paste* command to insert the picture wherever you want in your document.

What size?

If you want to alter the size of your inserted picture, use the I-beam to select it, and pick the *Size Picture* command from Write's *Edit* menu. The square pointer will appear again. This time, you can use it to stretch or shrink your picture.

Resizing an inserted picture

As you move the square pointer over one of the picture's borderlines, it will grab that borderline.

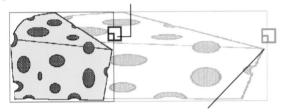

Move the borderline to the position you want. Then click to make the picture appear at this size.

Editing your picture

You might want to alter your picture after you have inserted it in your letter. To do this, select the picture with the I-beam and pick *Edit Paintbrush Picture Object* from Write's *Edit* menu. Alternatively, you can simply double-click on the picture with the I-beam.

A Paintbrush window containing your picture will appear. Use the Paintbrush controls to make any alterations. When you have finished, pick the *Update* command from the Paintbrush window's *File* menu. This tells your computer to replace the copy of the picture in your Write document with the altered version. Pick *Exit & Return to...* from the Paintbrush window's *File* menu to return to your document.

Saving a combined document

When you have finished your illustrated letter, use Write's Save As box to save it as a file on disk. Keep it with your other documents in the personal hard disk directory that you created on page 34. Because you have combined your letter and picture inside the Write window, use Write's filename extension, ".wri".

Other combinations

You can combine many of the other applications on your PC in much the same way as Write and Paintbrush. You could try using the Clipboard to insert Notepad notes into a Calendar schedule, or to move Paintbrush pictures into a Cardfile to produce an illustrated address book.

If your PC has extra application software for creating sounds or animation, you can even insert noises and moving pictures into your Windows documents.

HELP!

You can use an application's Help system to find out how to insert information created by other applications. Pages 44 and 45 explain how to use the Windows Help system.

How to get help

Windows includes its own set of instructions, called the Help system. As you explore an application, you can use the information in the Help system to tackle unfamiliar commands and controls, or to remind yourself of specific Windows techniques.

Calling for Help

To get help with a particular program, you have to make sure that its window is active. Then either press and release the **F1** key, or pick the _Contents_ command from the program's _Help_ menu. A Help window showing the program's Help Contents page will appear on your desktop.

This is the Contents page for Write's Help system.

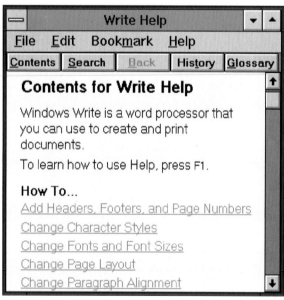

Choosing a topic

Once you have found the topic you want, point at its title in the Contents list. The pointer will turn into a hand shape like this:

By clicking on a topic title with the hand-shaped pointer, you can jump to the Help section which explains that topic. Whenever you want to return to the Help Contents page to choose a new topic, click on the _Contents_ button at the top of the Help window.

The Search button

Another way of finding information on a specific topic, is to use the Search option. Click on the Help window's _Search_ button and the dialog box below will appear on your desktop:

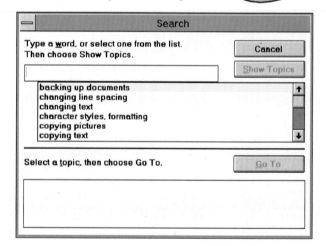

Help topics

Each program's Help instructions are organized into separate topics, as in an instruction manual. The Help Contents page lists these topics, showing each one as an underlined title. Use the scroll bar to look through the Contents list and find a topic which sounds as if it will cover the information you need.

Follow the instructions in the upper half of the Search box to specify the subject about which you need information. You can type it in, or scroll through the list of available subjects to find and highlight the one you want.

Once you have specified a subject, click on the _Show Topics_ button. All the Help topics relating to your chosen subject will appear in a list in the lower half of the Search box. Highlight the topic you want by clicking on it, then click on the _Go To_ button to jump to that Help topic.

The Glossary

Some of the more difficult computer words included in the Help instructions are underlined with a line of dashes. If you click the hand-shaped pointer on any of these words, a small box will appear containing a brief explanation of what that word means.

By clicking on the *Glossary* button you can browse through a list of all these computer words in a window on your desktop. Click the hand-shaped pointer on any word in the Glossary window to find out what it means.

This is the Glossary window, showing a sample definition.

	glossary	▼ ▲
	check box	↑
	choose	
	clear	
	click	

click

To press and release a mouse button quickly.

Back and History

Clicking on the *Back* button in a Help window takes you back to the Help page that you were using last. You can use this button to go back one page at a time through the Help pages that you have already used.

By clicking on the *History* button, you can open a window that lists all the Help pages you have used. To jump back to a particular topic, double-click on its title in the History list.

This is the Windows Help History window.

▬ Windows Help History
Inserting Drawings
Contents for Write Help
Changing Page Layout
Contents for Write Help
Changing Character Styles
Contents for Write Help

The topics are listed in the order in which you looked at them, with the most recent last.

HELP!
You can even use Help to find out how to use Help. Pick the *How to Use Help* command from the *Help* menu, or press the **F1** key twice in succession.

The Windows Tutorial

As well as the Help system, Windows includes a two-part lesson called the Windows Tutorial. The first part helps you learn the main mouse techniques (see page 11). The second part of the Tutorial, called Windows Basics, covers the skills introduced on pages 8 to 20 of this book.

To find the Tutorial, switch to Program Manager's window and pick *Windows Tutorial* from its *Help* menu. Press the **w** key to select Windows Basics.

You don't have to follow the lesson through from start to finish. You can flick backward or forward through its pages using the buttons at the bottom right-hand corner of the screen. By clicking on the *Contents* button, you can display the Tutorial Contents page and use a Topic button to jump to a particular section of the lesson.

This screen shows the Windows Tutorial Contents Page.

Contents

Click the button for the topic you want to learn about.

	Windows Basics Lessons
▫ Begin the Tutorial again	▫ Instructions
▫ Exit the Tutorial	▫ Starting an Application
	▫ Moving and Sizing Windows
Mouse Lesson	▫ Using Menus and Commands
▫ Begin Mouse Lesson	▫ Using Dialog Boxes
	▫ Switching Between Applications
	▫ Closing Applications

Return to the Tutorial To return to your current location in the Tutorial

Introducing Windows 95

Microsoft has developed a new operating system, called Windows 95. It is designed to be easier to use than earlier Windows software, and to enable PC users to take full advantage of advances in computer technology.

Windows 95 plays the same role as previous versions of Windows. It allows you to control your PC using a mouse pointer and pictures on your screen. Windows, icons, menus and dialog boxes all appear on the Windows 95 desktop.

However, there are several important ways in which Windows 95 differs from earlier Windows software.

The Start button

Program Manager is replaced in the Windows 95 system by a single button on the desktop, called the Start buttton.

By clicking on the Start button, you can open a menu that lists every program available on your computer. You can use this Start button menu to find and run the programs you want to use.

The Start button

The Taskbar

The Start button is found at one end of a narrow strip, called the Taskbar. The Taskbar can be positioned along any edge of the Windows 95 desktop. It is never hidden from view by other desktop items.

In addition to the Start button, the Taskbar includes a button for each program that your computer is currently running. By clicking a program's button on the Taskbar, you can bring that program's window to the top of the desktop. This provides a quick and easy way to switch between windows.

Part of the Taskbar

New gadgets

The Windows 95 desktop includes several new helpful gadgets, some of which you can see on the desktop on the right.

A Windows 95 desktop.

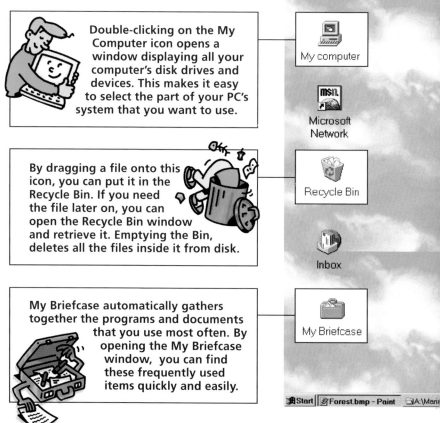

Double-clicking on the My Computer icon opens a window displaying all your computer's disk drives and devices. This makes it easy to select the part of your PC's system that you want to use.

By dragging a file onto this icon, you can put it in the Recycle Bin. If you need the file later on, you can open the Recycle Bin window and retrieve it. Emptying the Bin, deletes all the files inside it from disk.

My Briefcase automatically gathers together the programs and documents that you use most often. By opening the My Briefcase window, you can find these frequently used items quickly and easily.

A new filing system

File Manager is replaced in Windows 95 by a new filing system. Two separate programs, called File Find and Explorer, enable you to track down files, or reorganize them on disk.

Windows 95 filenames can be as long as you like. You don't need to add extensions to them (see page 22) because Windows 95 works out for itself which application was used to create each file.

Phileas File-Filington III Jnr.

Multitasking

Windows 95 enables your computer to do several different jobs at the same time. This is called multitasking. It means that you don't have to wait for your computer to finish one job before starting work on another.

The desktop below shows an example of multitasking. The user is playing cards with one program, while another program copies files.

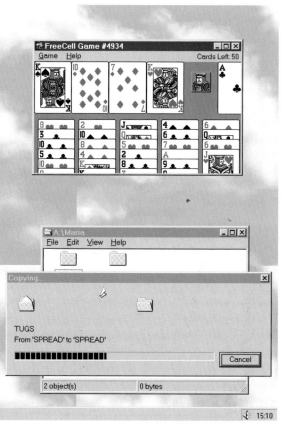

Multimedia advances

"Multimedia" means using a computer to combine text, sound, pictures and video to present information.

Advances in computer technology mean that PCs are becoming better and better at handling multimedia.

The Windows 95 system is designed so that you can work with different kinds of information easily and effectively. It enables you to use your PC to run existing multimedia "presentations", or even to create your own.

Joining the network

A group of computers linked together so that they can exchange information is called a network.

PCs can be connected with other PCs nearby to form a local area network. They can even be connected over long distances, via the telephone system, to form a wide area network. Some wide area computer networks stretch all the way around the world.

Windows 95 has several features to help you use networks. The Network Neighborhood program enables your PC to function as part of a local area network. Another program, called The Microsoft Network, lets you join and use Microsoft's own international PC network.

All the information that your computer has recently received from the network is gathered together in the "Inbox" on the Windows 95 desktop.

Windows words

The list below explains some of the unusual words that you'll come across as you read or talk about Microsoft Windows. Words printed in *italics* are explained elsewhere in the list.

If you come across any other unfamiliar Windows words, try looking them up in the Glossary included in the Windows Help system. You can find out how to use the Glossary on page 45.

Active The word used to describe a *window* that is currently in use.

Button Part of the *desktop* that you can "press" with the *pointer* to enter a command.

Cascading A way of arranging *windows* on the *desktop* so that they are neatly stacked.

Clicking Pressing the primary *mouse* button to "touch" an item on the *desktop*.

Clipboard The part of the Windows system which stores information temporarily, so that it can be transferred from one place to another.

Closing Removing a *window* from the *desktop* when it is no longer required.

Desktop The screen display used to control Windows.

Dialog box A rectangular area on the *desktop*, rather like a *window*, containing various controls used to enter choices.

Directory tree A diagram in the *File Manager* window showing how files are organized on disk.

Disabled The word used to describe a *menu* command or *button* which is temporarily unresponsive to *clicking*.

Double-clicking Pressing the primary *mouse* button twice in quick succession, usually to activate a *desktop* shortcut.

Dragging Pressing and holding down the primary *mouse* button to grab an item on the *desktop* in order to move it around.

File Manager The part of the Windows system used to find and organize files.

Help system The built-in instruction manual included in the Windows software.

I-beam The I-shaped *pointer* used to position the *insertion point* and select text.

Icon A small picture on the *desktop*, representing part of the Windows system.

Inactive The word used to describe a *window* which is displayed on the *desktop*, but is not currently being used.

Insertion point The flashing line showing the position where text is to be inserted in a document.

Maximizing Enlarging a *window* to fill the entire *desktop*.

Menu A list of Windows commands grouped together under a specific heading.

Menu bar A horizontal strip beneath a window's *title bar* used to select a particular *menu*.

Minimizing Converting a *window* to an *icon*.

Mouse A hand-held device used to control the *pointer*, and so operate the Windows system.

Opening Bringing a new *window* onto the *desktop*.

Pointer The movable on-screen arrow, controlled with the *mouse*, which is used to operate the *desktop*.

Program Manager The part of the Windows system used to find and run a particular program.

Restoring Returning a *window* to its original size and position on the *desktop*.

Scrolling Shifting a *window*'s view, using its scroll bars, until it displays a specific area of its contents.

Switching Using the *Task List* or special keystrokes to select a particular *window* from those on the *desktop*.

Task List A specialized *dialog box* for tidying the *desktop* or switching to a specific *window*.

Tiling A way of arranging *windows* on the *desktop* so that they fit neatly beside each other.

Title bar A strip across the top of a *window* showing its name.

Wallpaper The patterned layer covering the *desktop*.

Window A rectangular area on the *desktop* providing a workspace in which to use a particular program.

PROJECTS FOR WINDOWS®
FOR BEGINNERS

Program
Manager

Recorder

Object
Packager

Cardfile

Control
Panel

Philippa Wingate

**Illustrated by Derek Matthews,
Jonathan Satchell and Nick Baxter**

File Manager

Paintbrush

Sound
Recorder

Write

Character
Map

Designed by Paul Greenleaf and Neil Francis
Russell Punter, Non Figg and Rachel Wells

Technical Consultant: Richard Payne

Edited by Anthony Marks and Jane Chisholm

Contents

What is this section about?

This section of the book shows you how to use the applications included free with Windows software to tackle a variety of projects. These projects include customizing your Windows display with new colors and patterns; making personalized stationary and greeting cards and creating cryptic codes and quiz games.

The main applications you will need to use are Control Panel, Write, Paintbrush, Cardfile, Character Map, Recorder and Object Packager.

Versions and updates

The projects in this section of the book are demonstrated using Windows 3.1.

If you don't have this version of Windows installed on your computer, don't panic. You will still be able to complete the projects if your computer has any of the following versions installed: Windows 3.11 or Windows® for Workgroups 3.1 and 3.11.

Tackle the projects with these versions of Windows.

Windows 95

You may have Windows® 95 installed on your computer (see pages 46 and 47). This version of Windows is fairly different to version 3.1. Find out about more of the differences on pages 94 and 95.

Using this section

To use this section of the book you will use the knowledge you have already gained about Windows applications. However, some brief reminders of how to operate the main applications are included.

Each project is described with clear, step-by-step instructions. The projects get more complicated toward the end of the book, so it's a good idea to work your way through from beginning to end.

Essential equipment

To complete many of the projects in this book all you need is a computer and Windows software. The book assumes that your Windows software has been installed in a "typical" way. The project instructions are written for a right-handed mouse user.

To print pictures and letters, you will need a printer. If you don't have a color printer, make sure you have pens or paints to decorate your printouts.

If you want to send project files to your friends, you'll need floppy disks to transfer the files.

This is the only equipment you'll need to tackle most of the projects in this book.

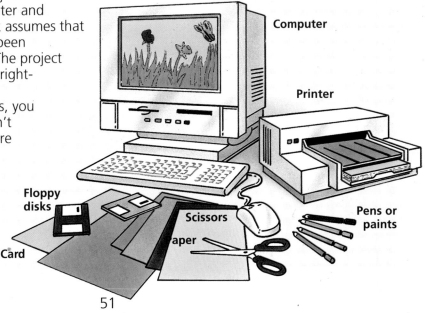

Computer

Printer

Floppy disks

Scissors

Pens or paints

aper

Card

51

A reminder of Windows basics

These two pages include a brief reminder about the different parts of a Windows display, how to control a window and how to open and close an application.

All this information is explained in greater detail in the first section of this book.

Windows, icons and your desktop

A basic Windows display is made up of windows, icons and a background layer called the desktop. The picture below shows you some of the main parts of a Windows display and tells you their names.

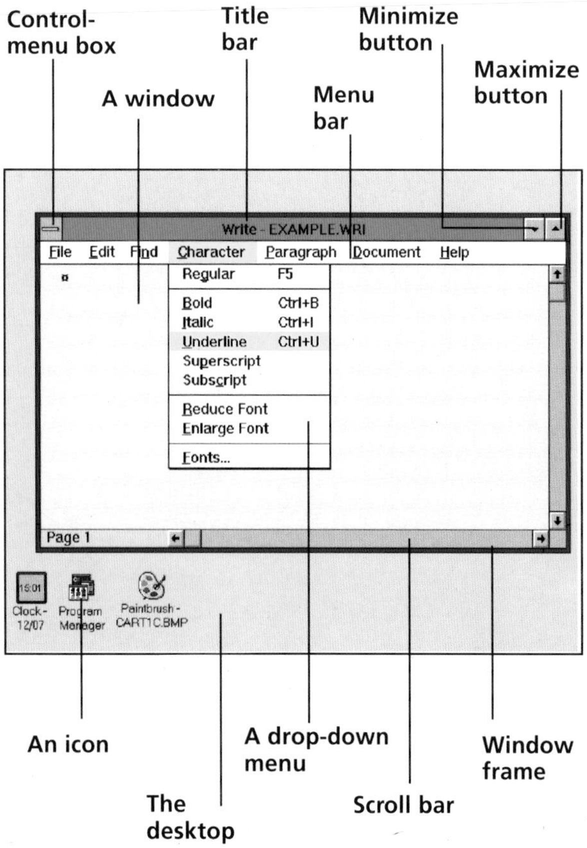

Control-menu box

Title bar

Minimize button

A window

Menu bar

Maximize button

| Write - EXAMPLE.WRI |
| File Edit Find Character Paragraph Document Help |

Regular   F5

Bold   Ctrl+B
Italic   Ctrl+I
Underline   Ctrl+U
Superscript
Subscript

Reduce Font
Enlarge Font

Fonts...

Page 1

Clock - 12/07   Program Manager   Paintbrush - CART1C.BMP

An icon

A drop-down menu

Window frame

The desktop

Scroll bar

Program Manager

When you first start up Windows 3.1, a window called Program Manager appears on your screen. If it appears as an icon at the bottom of your screen, double-click on it to open the window.

This is the Program Manager icon.

All the instructions for the projects in this book start from Program Manager. For these instructions to work properly, you need open Program Manager's *Options* menu and click on *Minimize on Use*, so that a check mark appears beside it, as in the picture below.

Options
Auto Arrange
√ Minimize on Use
Save Settings on Exit

To select an item, click on it in the menu.

Opening an application

All the applications on your computer are grouped together in program groups inside the Program Manager window.

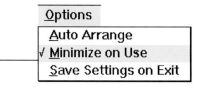

This is a program group icon.

Games

To open a program group, double-click on its icon. A new window will open inside Program Manager. It will contain the icons of all the applications in that particular group.

Each standard Windows application has a different icon. An icon usually gives you an idea of what its application is used for. For example, this icon is for File Manager, which is an application used to organize the files on your computer. The icon looks like a filing cabinet.

To open an application, simply double-click your pointer on its icon.

Resizing a window

When an application opens, a window appears on your screen containing the workspace in which you use the application. You can change the shape of the window by clicking on its frame and dragging it into the shape you want.

To make a window fill your whole screen, click on its Maximize button.

This window is being resized to a smaller size.

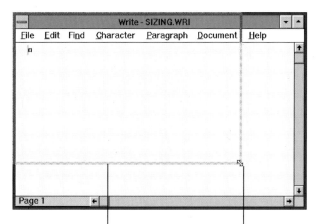

This outline shows you the new size of the window.

With this resizing pointer, drag the window into the shape you want.

Minimizing applications

You can have several applications running on your computer at once. To make sure that you have enough space on your desktop to use an application properly, it's a good idea to minimize the windows of other applications. To do this, click on their Minimize buttons. They will appear as icons at the bottom of your screen. They are still running, and you can "restore" them to their former size, by double-clicking on their icons.

Closing an application

If you have finished using an application and want to close it down completely, select *Exit* in the application's *File* menu. Another, quicker way of closing an application is to double-click in its control-menu box.

Directories

All the files stored on a computer's hard disk are grouped together in directories. Make a new directory for the files you will create while doing the projects in this book. This will keep them separate from all the other information on your computer.

Creating a new directory

To create a "projects" directory, open the File Manager application by double-clicking on its icon in Program Manager. Inside its window there will be one or more windows. Close all but one of these windows. Select *Select Drive* in the *Disk* menu and in the dialog box highlight the hard disk drive (usually the C drive). The window will now display the directories on the hard disk.

Click on the folder symbol at the top of the list which has C:\ written next to it (see below). Select *Create Directory...* in the *File* menu. A Create Directory dialog box will appear. In the *Name* box, type PROJECTS and click *OK*. A projects directory will appear in the list. Find out how to put files into this directory on page 60.

File Manager's window with a projects directory

The C:\ folder symbol

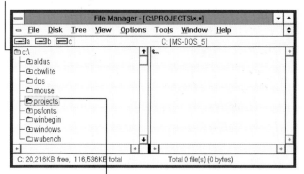

Your new directory appears in this list.

Be careful

Make sure that you don't delete or change any files already stored on the hard disk of the computer you are using.

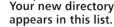

Changing your Windows display

If you have a color monitor, the desktop, windows and icons which make up a Windows display will be multicolored. If you have a black and white monitor, the display will be black, white and shades of grey. You can change the appearance of your display using the programs found in the Control Panel application.

Control Panel

Control Panel is usually found in the program group called Main. Open it by double-clicking on its icon in the Program Manager window.

 This is the Control Panel icon.

Things to avoid

When using Control Panel avoid the following programs: Network, Ports, Keyboard, International, 386 Enhanced, Drivers. They won't alter the appearance of your display, and changing them could cause problems with your computer hardware.

Avoid these icons in Control Panel.

Printers

International

Ports

Keyboard

386 Enhanced

Drivers

Changing color schemes

To change the color schemes of the windows and desktop that make up your Windows display, double-click on the Color icon in the Control Panel window.

This is the Color icon.

In the Color window that appears, open the *Color Schemes* list. It contains a selection of color combinations, with names like Arizona, Tweed or Hotdog Stand. Try one out by highlighting its name in the list. The sample display below the list will change to show you what your chosen color scheme looks like.

The sample Windows display in this Color window is showing a scheme called Patchwork.

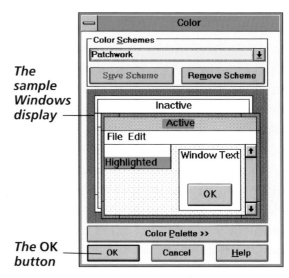

The sample Windows display

The OK button

When you have found a scheme you like, click the *OK* button. The Color window will close and the display will show your new colors.

Choosing your own colors

If you don't like any of the existing Windows color schemes, you can create your own. In the Color window, click on the *Color Palette>>* button. The window will extend to show a palette of colors.

The Basic Colors *palette*

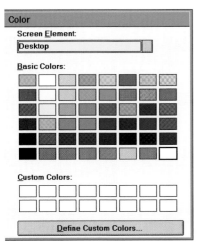

Click on any element of the sample Windows display, such as the "Active Title Bar" or the "Menu Bar". The name of the element you have selected will appear in the *Screen Element* box. Now choose a new color for this element by clicking on any of the colored squares in the *Basic Colors* palette.

Mixing colors

Like an artist, you can mix up your own selection of dazzling new colors.

To do this, click on an empty square in the *Custom Colors* section. Click the *Define Custom Colors...* button. A dialog box appears containing a multicolored square. Select the color in any part of the square by clicking on it. To add this color to your palette, click the *Add Color* button. To close the Custom Color Selector box, click the *Close* button.

The Custom Color Selector box

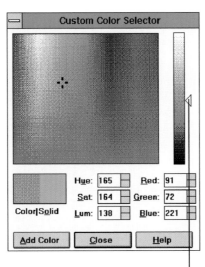

Drag this pointer up and down to change the brightness of your new color.

Saving a scheme

When you have designed a color scheme that you are happy with, you need to save it. In the Color window, click the *Save Scheme* button. A dialog box appears. Type in a name for your scheme, such as Blue Boomerang or Peachy Pig Pink and click *OK*.

Displaying a scheme

To display your colors on screen, close the Color window by clicking the *OK* button at the bottom left-hand corner of the window. Your personal color scheme will automatically appear on the screen.

Black and white

If you have a black and white monitor you can still change the appearance of your display. There are different shades and textures to choose from in the *Color Palette* dialog box.

Some of the schemes in the *Color Schemes* list begin with the letters LCD. These combinations are specially designed for use on monochrome monitors and laptop computers. Try some of them out using the technique described above.

Customizing your desktop

There are other ways in which you can change the Windows display. You can change the pattern that decorates the desktop using the Control Panel application.

How to see your desktop

To make sure that you can see the desktop of your Windows display, double-click on the Control Panel icon in Program Manager.

This is the Desktop icon. Double-click on it and the Desktop window will appear. In this window there is a section called Wallpaper. Open up the *File* list and highlight *(None)*.

The Wallpaper section of the Desktop window

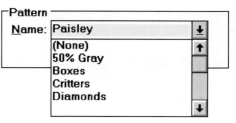

When you click *OK* in the top right-hand corner of the Desktop window, you will be able to see the desktop at the back of your screen.

Coloring your desktop

To change the color of your desktop, use the Color program in Control Panel. You can read about how to change the color elements of your display on page 54 and 55. Select the desktop on the sample Windows display and assign it a new color in the *Color Palette*.

Patterns on your desktop

The patterns which you can choose to decorate your desktop are made up of small patterns repeated hundreds of times to fill your screen.

In the section of the Desktop window called Pattern, open the *Name* list. This shows you all the desktop patterns provided by Windows.

The Pattern section of the Desktop window

To try out one of the patterns, such as Boxes or Scottie, highlight its name in the *File* list. Click the *OK* button and your desktop background will immediately change.

Two of Window's desktop patterns.

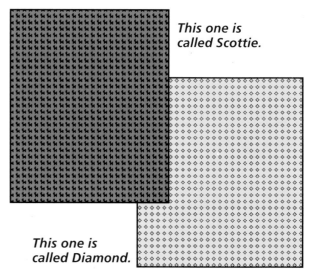

This one is called Scottie.

This one is called Diamond.

How to design your own desktop pattern

If you don't like any of the existing desktop patterns provided by Windows, you can design your own. In the Desktop window, open the _Name_ list in the Pattern section and select _(None)_. Click the _Edit Pattern..._ button and a dialog box will open.

In the Edit Pattern dialog box there are two empty boxes. The larger one is covered with lots of invisible squares. When you click anywhere in this square with your pointer, a small black square will appear. If you click on it again, the small black square will disappear.

This is the Edit Pattern dialog box.

The name of your pattern.

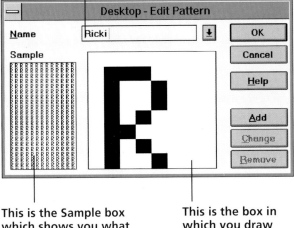

This is the Sample box which shows you what your pattern will look like.

This is the box in which you draw your pattern.

Using this technique create new shapes and patterns by adding black boxes. As you change the pattern, you can see the effect it will have on your desktop in the box called Sample.

Changing existing patterns

You can also change some of the existing desktop patterns. Select one of them and then click on _Edit Pattern..._ Using your pointer, alter the pattern of the black squares.

**A selection of the patterns you can create.**

You can use a letter.

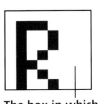

The box in which the pattern is drawn.

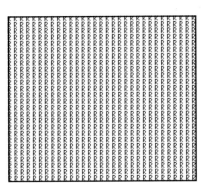

Stripes look good.

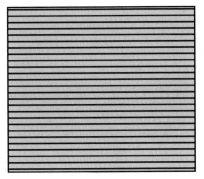

Naming your pattern

When you have created a pattern that you like and want to keep, give it a name in the _Name_ box, such as Stripes or Rings. Then click the _Add_ button.

To close the Desktop - Edit Pattern dialog box, click the _OK_ button. When you do this, you will immediately see your new pattern covering the desktop.

Super screen savers

If you leave the same image displayed on your screen for a long time, it becomes permanently imprinted on the screen glass. This is called screen burn. To avoid it, you can use a program called screen saver, which replaces the image with a moving picture after a certain amount of time. Windows provides a selection of different moving images that you can alter and personalize.

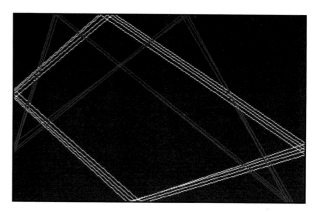

Windows has a screen saver called Mystify.

Turning on a screen saver

To choose a Windows screen saver, double-click on the Control Panel icon in Program Manager. In the Control Panel window, double-click on the Desktop icon. There is a section of the Desktop window called Screen Saver. Open the *Name* list and you will find a list of screen savers available on your computer.

This is the Screen Saver dialog box

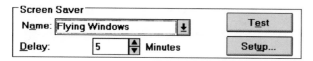

Try out one of them, say Flying Windows, by highlighting its name and then clicking on the *Test* button. If you use the Flying Windows screen saver, your screen will change to show lots of Windows logos rushing toward you.

A screen showing Flying Windows screen saver

Stopping a screen saver

Screen savers are designed to disappear from the screen the moment you move your mouse or press any of the keys on the keyboard. Stop the test demonstration of a screen saver by doing either of these things.

Setting a delay time

You can instruct your computer to start a screen saver automatically when you leave it unused for a certain amount of time. By clicking on the upward or the downward arrows on the right-hand side of the *Delay* box, you can alter the number of minutes your computer is idle before the screen saver is activated.

Making changes

You can alter the colors and speed of some of the Windows screen savers. To do this, highlight the screen saver you want to alter in the *Name* list. Click the *Setup...* button and a Setup dialog box will appear.

This is the Mystify Setup dialog box.

Make sure *Active* is selected.

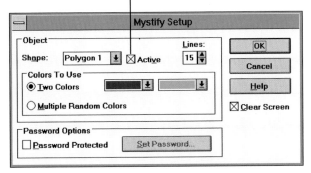

With the Mystify screen saver, for example, you can change the shape, color and the number of lines which make up the shapes, called polygons, that appear on your screen.

You can decide whether the screen goes black when the screen saver starts or whether the polygons gradually black out the screen. When you have selected your preferences, click *OK*.

Personal messages

If you choose to use the Marquee screen saver, you can write a message that will travel across your screen. Select a color for the letters and the background. Type in your message in the *Text* box section. You can also choose the speed at which the words will travel. Finally, click *OK*.

This is the Marquee Setup dialog box.

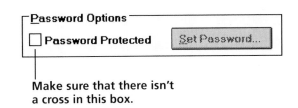

Passwords

In the Setup boxes of each screen saver you are given the option of putting a password on your screen saver. This means that when the screen saver comes on it will remain "locked" on the screen until you type in a special password.

It's not a good idea to put a password on your screen saver. You might forget the password and nobody would be able to use the computer until a computer expert unlocked the screen saver.

Click your pointer in the box beside *Password Protected* in the *Password Options* section until there is no cross in the box.

This is the P̲assword Options section.

┌ **P̲assword Options** ────────────────────
│ ☐ **Password Protected**   Set Password...

Make sure that there isn't a cross in this box.

Ready to go

When you have selected the screen saver you want, click the *OK* button and close the Control Panel window by double-clicking in its control-menu box.

Your screen saver is now activated. Whenever you leave your computer for the period of time you have specified, the screen saver will appear.

A Write reminder

You will need to use the Write application in many of the projects in this book, so here's a reminder of some of its main features. To open Write, double-click on its icon in Program Manager.

This is the Write icon.

A window opens containing a blank page. A flashing cursor in the left-hand corner indicates where your text appears when you start typing.

This is a Write window.

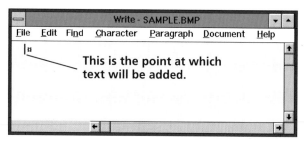

This is the point at which text will be added.

Saving a Write file

When you have typed in some text, such as a letter or a story, you should save your Write document. Open the *File* menu and select *Save As...* The following dialog box will appear.

A Save As dialog box

Type in the name of your file here.

Select the directory in which you want to store your file.

File Name:	Directories:	OK
letter3.wri	c:\projects	Cancel
letter1.wri	🗁 c:\	
letter2.wri	🗁 projects	☐ Backup
Save File as Type:	Drives:	
Write Files (*.WRI)	💾 c: ms-dos_5	

Select the Write Files (*.WRI) option here.

Select a drive to store your file on here.

Type a filename in the *File Name* box. It can have up to eight letters or numbers. All Write files have the extension .WRI. So select *.WRI in the *Save File as Type* box. In the *Drives* list highlight the disk drive which contains the disk you want to save your file on.

 Floppy disk drives have icons like this beside them.

 The hard disk drive (usually the C drive) has an icon like this.

To put your file into your projects directory (see page 53), double-click on the C:\ folder at the top of the *Directories* list. In the list that appears, double-click on the projects directory and then click *OK*.

This method of saving a file is similar to the technique you will use to save and store any file created in a Windows application.

Printing out a Write file

To print out a Write file, you need to have a printer installed and connected to your computer. Make sure that it is switched on and "on line", which means that it is ready to receive data from your computer.

Select *Open...* in Write's *File* menu. In the dialog box highlight the name of the file you want to print. Click *OK* and the document will appear in Write's window.

Select *Print Setup...* in the *File* menu. Check that the type of printer you are using is specified in the Printer section. In the Paper section, check that the size of the paper you are using is highlighted. Then click *OK*.

Select *Print...* in Write's *File* menu. If your document has more than one page, specify which pages you want to print. Enter the number of copies of your document you want. Finally, click *OK* to begin printing.

Letterheads

You don't have to type your name and address at the top of every letter you send. You can store this information in a Write document called a letterhead.

Creating a letterhead

Open a copy of Write and type in the information you want in your letterhead. This usually includes your name, address, telephone and fax number, but you may want to include other information too.

A selection of printed letterheads and notepaper

Arranging text

You can arrange your letterhead information wherever you like on the page. To arrange any text, you must highlight it first. To do this, click your cursor at the beginning of the block of text you want to arrange and drag it to the end. Release the mouse button, and your text will appear highlighted, like **this**.

Highlight your letterhead information in this way, and in the *Paragraph* menu select *Left*, *Right* or *Centered*, depending on where you want your text to appear on the page.

Saving your letterhead

When you are ready, select *Save As...* in Write's *File* menu. Give your file a name (letrhead.wri, for example). Place it in your projects directory and save it.

To write a letter, open letrhead.wri and type in your message underneath the letterhead information. Select *Save As...* in the *File* menu and give your letter a new filename (such as letter.wri). This will ensure that your letterhead file remains unaltered.

Brighter letters

When you print out a letter, you can add some color and patterns to it with pens or paints. In the picture below, the letterheads have been printed on colored paper. Bright patterns and borders have been added. You can make your own notepaper by printing your letterhead file onto several sheets of paper and adding a handwritten note.

More news on using Write

You can use Write to create leaflets or newsletters. By exploring the different styles and shapes of text available and varying the size and position of your text, you can produce professional-looking documents.

Using different text styles

One way of making text easier to read and understand is to use different text styles to emphasize important information. Write's *Character* menu provides a selection of text styles from which you can choose. Each one alters the appearance of text on the page, making it stand out from ordinary type. The different styles available are:

Bold, which makes text darker.

Italic, which makes text lean to the right.

<u>Underline</u>, which puts a line underneath text.

To use any of these styles, highlight the block of text you wish to alter (see page 61). Then select *Bold, Italic* or *Underline* in the *Character* menu.

A letter showing different text styles in Write

Fonts

A font is a set of letters, numbers or symbols which have a unique shape and appearance.

THIS IS A FONT CALLED "BOSANOVA".

This is a font called "Briquet".

Stored on a computer is a selection of fonts that you can use to produce a document. Some fonts are provided with Windows software, but you can also increase the range of fonts on your computer by buying extra software.

Trying out different fonts

Open Write and type in some text. Highlight the text you want to change to a different font. In the *Character* menu select *Fonts...* A Fonts dialog box opens like the one below.

A Fonts dialog box

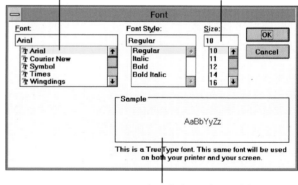

The *Font* list

Change the size of your text here.

A sample of the selected font

If you select a font in the *Font* list, a sample of it appears in the Sample box. When you have found one you like, click *OK* and your text will appear in the new font.

You can also change the size of highlighted text by changing the number in the *Size* section of the Font dialog box. The higher the number, the larger your text.

This text is size 18.

This text is the same font, but size 12.

Making your own newsletter

Newspapers use a variety of different text styles and fonts. You may also have noticed that the text is usually arranged in narrow columns. You can use all these techniques to produce a newsletter like the one shown here.

A narrow column of text

To create a narrow column of text, select *Ruler On* in the *Document* menu. A ruler appears at the top of your page. At the left-hand end of the Ruler is a triangular marker. This indicates the left-hand edge of your text column.

At the right-hand end of the ruler is another marker marking the right-hand edge of your text column. Click your cursor on it and drag it toward the left-hand side of your page. Using the measurements on the Ruler, position this triangle at the column width you require.

Now, when you type in your news story, it will appear in a neat column.

A narrow column of text in Write

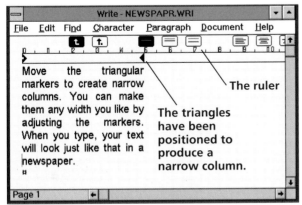

Move the triangular markers to create narrow columns. You can make them any width you like by adjusting the markers. When you type, your text will look just like that in a newspaper.

The triangles have been positioned to produce a narrow column.

The ruler

Justified text

Many newspapers use justified text. This means that the words in each line have been spaced out to fill the width of the column. To make your text justified, highlight it and select *Justified* in the *Paragraph* menu.

Summer Vacation

In July we... way for our sum... ation. The who... g was... saster... a crash... the airport... managed to... e to catch... y sister... never flown... d she loved ev... y minute of it.

The flight took ten hours and we had three meals on the plane.

This is Jessica and I at the airport.

Lots of shells

The first morning we were in Spain Jessica and I decided to explore the beach. There were lots of different things that the tide had washed up. We collected a whole selection of stones, glass, bones and shells to take home with us.

Some of the shells we found.

Diving in

I learned to dive in the pool at the hotel, keeping my legs straight.

This is me diving in to the pool.

Banana crazy

On Monday we went to the beach again. We went for a ride on a huge banana. A speed boat pulled it really fast and we all found it very difficult to hang on.

At first, you think it is going to be really easy to stay on, because the man in the speed boat pulling the banana goes slowly. When he goes faster, however, the waves make you bounce up and down and the rubber banana gets so slippery that it is almost impossible to hang on.

Places we visited

There were lots of places to visit near the hotel. W... went to a park w... there were some...

A vacation photograph

It was a Roman settlement. There were lots of mosaics on the ground and some of the wa... were still standi... We b... famou... found I...

To make your newsletter more colorful, you can use felt-tip pens or stick in photographs.

Finishing

When you have printed out a selection of stories for your newsletter, paste them onto a large sheet of paper. Add lines to divide the columns of text and draw some pictures. When it is ready, photocopy and distribute your newsletter.

ALIENS HAVE LANDED

A recap on Paintbrush

 This is the icon for Paintbrush. You can read all about this application on pages 26 to 29, but here is a brief reminder of how to use it.

A Paintbrush window

The Toolbox has 18 drawing tools that create different effects.

This is the canvas area where you draw your picture.

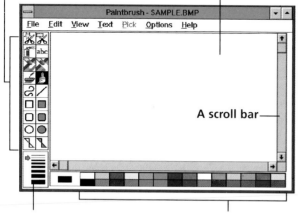

A scroll bar

The Linesize box allows you to select the width of your tools.

The Palette of colors

Sizing your canvas

To create a canvas of a particular size, select *Image Attributes...* in the *Options* menu. A dialog box appears like the one below:

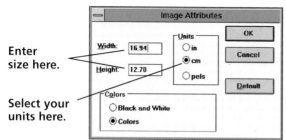

Enter size here.

Select your units here.

Type in the width and height of the canvas you require in the boxes. Make sure that centimeters is selected in the *Units* section. When you click *OK*, your canvas changes size.

If the canvas you are working on is too large to fit in Paintbrush's window, scroll bars will appear. By clicking on them, you can move around the whole canvas area.

Choosing new colors

There are two main types of color in Paintbrush: the foreground color and the background color. The foreground color is the one you use to draw things. The background color is the color of the canvas on which you are drawing.

To pick a foreground color, click on a color in the Palette with your left-hand mouse button. To select a background color, click with your right-hand mouse button. The box at the left-hand end of the Palette shows the colors currently selected for the foreground and background.

Part of the Paintbrush Palette

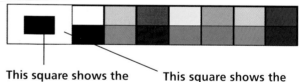

This square shows the foreground color.

This square shows the background color.

Creating a picture

You can use any of the tools in Paintbrush's Toolbox to draw a picture. To select a new tool, click on its icon in the panel. To paint with it, drag your cursor over the canvas area. The best way to find out how all the different tools work is to experiment with them. Some of the more complicated tools are explained in greater detail in the projects where you need to use them.

Erasing mistakes

You can correct any mistakes you make when drawing a Paintbrush picture. Highlight the Eraser tool and move it over the area you want to erase.

This is the Eraser tool icon.

Alternatively, select *Undo* in the *Edit* menu, to undo everything you have done since you chose a new tool or color.

Saving a picture

To save a Paintbrush picture, select *Save As...* in the *File* menu. The dialog box below appears.

The Save As dialog box

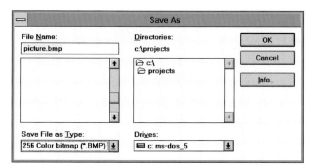

Give your picture a filename. Paintbrush filenames are always given the extension .BMP, so select *.BMP in the *Save File as Type* box. Place it in the projects directory and save it.

New pictures

When you want to start a new canvas, simply select *New* in the *File* menu. A new canvas will automatically appear. It will be exactly the same size as the one you used previously.

Printing out a picture

If you have a printer installed and connected to your computer and it is on line, you can print out a Paintbrush picture. To do this, select *Open...* in the *File* menu. Select the name of the file you want to print and click *OK*. Select *Print...* from the *File* menu. A Print dialog box appears, containing a selection of print options.

This is the Print dialog box.

For the best quality printing, select *Proof*.

In this section you can choose to print a small area of your picture, or all of it.

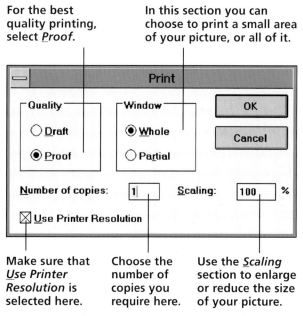

Make sure that *Use Printer Resolution* is selected here.

Choose the number of copies you require here.

Use the *Scaling* section to enlarge or reduce the size of your picture.

To make sure that your picture is printed as clearly as possible, select *Proof* in the *Quality* section. Make sure that *Whole* is selected in the *Window* section. This will ensure that all of your picture is printed, not just the area you can see in the Paintbrush window.

Type in the number of copies of your picture you want to print. Use the *Scaling* section to specify the size at which you want your picture to be printed out.

When you are ready, click the *OK* button to begin printing.

65

Design your own wallpaper

You can cover your desktop with a layer of patterns or pictures called wallpaper. Choose a wallpaper from the patterns Windows provides, or design your own.

Choosing a new wallpaper

To choose a wallpaper for your screen, double-click on the Control Panel icon in Program Manager. Then double-click on the Desktop icon. In the Desktop window there is a Wallpaper section.

To ensure that the wallpaper you are about to choose appears all over the back of your screen, click in the circle beside *Tile* until a dot appears.

The Wallpaper section

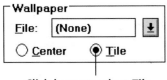

Click here to select *Tile*.

Now open the *File* list which contains the names of all the Windows wallpapers. They have names such as cars.bmp or zigzag.bmp. Try out one of them by highlighting it and clicking *OK*. The Desktop window will close and the new wallpaper will appear at the back of your screen.

These screens show two of the Windows wallpapers

This one is called leaves.bmp.

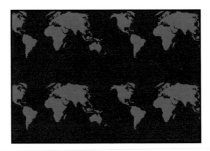

This one is called world.bmp.

Customizing

To alter a Windows wallpaper, open a copy of Paintbrush. Select *Open...* in the *File* menu.

In the dialog box that appears, select the windows directory in the *Directories* section. Then, in the *File Name* section, select the name of the wallpaper you want to alter. When you click *OK*, part of that wallpaper will appear on your canvas. You can add colors and patterns to it.

Color Eraser

A useful tool for customizing wallpaper is the Color Eraser. Select it by clicking on its icon in the Toolbox.

This is the Color Eraser icon.

The Color Eraser allows you to change the colors in a picture without altering the pattern. For example, if you don't like the blue areas of a wallpaper design, select that blue in the Palette with your left-hand mouse button. Select the color you would like to replace it with, say red, with the right-hand mouse button. Then, hold down the left-hand button and, with your cursor, shade over the wallpaper design on your canvas.

Using Color Eraser

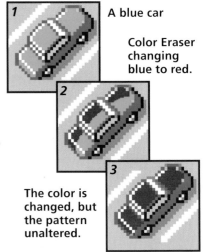

1   A blue car

Color Eraser changing blue to red.

2

3

The color is changed, but the pattern unaltered.

Make sure that the original wallpaper file remains unaltered by saving your new wallpaper file under a different filename.

Make your own wallpaper

You can design your own wallpaper using Paintbrush. A wallpaper appears on your desktop in tiles. The number of tiles that are needed to cover the desktop depends on the size of the canvas you use to create a wallpaper. If you draw on a small canvas (say, about 2cm by 2cm), it will be repeated many times to cover your desktop. If you choose a larger canvas (say, 6cm by 6cm), it will only be repeated a few times.

Open Paintbrush and select *Image Attributes...* in the *Options* menu. Enter the measurements of the canvas you require and click *OK*.

Two sample wallpaper designs

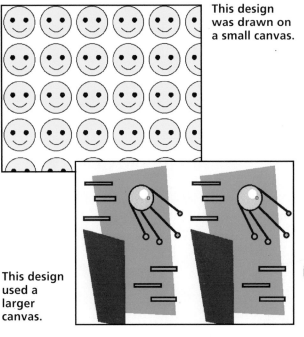

This design was drawn on a small canvas.

This design used a larger canvas.

Design a tile of wallpaper using any of the tools and colors Paintbrush offers. The Paintbrush window below shows a large tile of wallpaper.

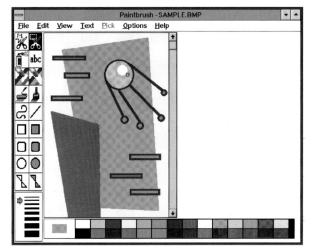

Naming wallpaper files

When you have finished your wallpaper design, you need to save it. Click on *Save As...* in Paintbrush's *File* menu. Give your wallpaper a filename with a .BMP extension. Put it in the directory on your hard disk called windows and save it. Close Paintbrush by double-clicking in its control-menu box.

Redecorating

To "paste" your wallpaper onto your desktop, open Control Panel and double-click on the Desktop icon. In the Wallpaper section, open the *File* list and select your newly named wallpaper file in the windows directory. When you click *OK*, your design will appear on screen.

Greetings and invitations

Use Paintbrush to create pictures you can mount on cardboard to make greeting cards and party invitations.

Getting started

Open Paintbrush and select *Image Attributes...* in the *Options* menu. Specify a canvas that is about 12cm wide and 17cm high. Click *OK* and your canvas will appear.

When you draw your picture, use the scroll bars (see page 64) to fill the whole of your canvas.

Some pictures drawn in Paintbrush

Outlined shapes

If you don't have a printer that prints in color, create a design made up of outlined shapes that you can color in after the picture is printed out. These are the icons for the tools which create outlined shapes.

A section of Paintbrush's Toolbox

Give your shapes a clear outline by selecting a wide tool width in the Linesize box.

This picture uses many of the outline tools.

Lettering in Paintbrush

This is the icon for the Text tool. You can use it to add text to a picture. There is a selection of different fonts, text sizes and styles to choose from. (You can read more about fonts and styles on page 62.)

To add text to a picture, select the Text tool. Open the *Text* menu and you will see the options of *Bold, Italic* or *Underline*. If you select *Fonts...*, a dialog box will appear in which you can alter the font and size of your text. Click on your canvas and start typing.

You could make a card using different fonts and sizes.

Mistakes

If you want to change some text in a Paintbrush picture, use the Eraser tool to erase it and then start again.

If you make a mistake while you are typing, you can use the backspace key to erase the mistake, then retype your text correctly.

Zoom in

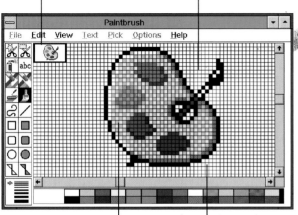

If you want to draw a picture carefully and precisely, try using a technique called "zooming in".

When you select *Zoom In* in the *View* menu, your pointer becomes a rectangle. Move this rectangle to the area of your picture you want a closer look at. Click, and the display will change to show that area in more detail.

When you are ready, select *Zoom Out* in the *View* menu to go back to the normal view of your canvas.

Making changes

This is the Brush tool's icon. When you have zoomed in on an area of a picture, you can use this tool to add detail to your picture, square by square. If you want to correct a mistake in a picture, add squares of the background color by clicking in the squares with your right-hand mouse button.

Looking at a detail of a picture using Zoom In

This box shows you the area you are altering, at its normal size.

The magnified area of your canvas

Click on each square or drag your pointer over them to add color.

Add background color if you want to delete mistakes.

Finishing touches

When the picture for your greeting card is finished, select *Save As...* in the *File* menu. Give your file a name (say, card.bmp), place it in the projects directory and save it.

Print out your picture onto a piece of paper. Mount it on a piece of cardboard that has been folded in half. Use paints, colored pencils or felt tips to color it in.

Some cards for a birthday party

The personal touch

Many companies have a symbol or picture, called a "logo", which helps people to identify them or their products. Using Paintbrush you can create your own distinctive logo.

Creating a logo

Open a copy of Paintbrush by double-clicking on its icon in Program Manager. Select *Image Attributes...* in the *Options* menu. Create a canvas about 4cm in width and 4cm in height, and then click *OK*. Now draw your logo, using any of the tools and paints.

Here is a selection of different logo ideas.

When you have created your logo, select *Save As...* in the *File* menu, give your file a name (say, logo.bmp), place it in the projects directory and save it.

Some logos on letterheads and personal cards

Using your logo

You could add your logo to the letterhead you created on page 61. Open the Paintbrush file containing your logo and select the Scissor tool.

This is the Scissor tool icon.

Use it to draw a dotted line around your logo, as shown below. Select *Copy* from the *Edit* menu. Close this copy of Paintbrush by double-clicking in its control-menu box.

Cutting out your logo

The cutting line created by the Scissor tool

This is the area that will be cut out.

Inserting a logo

Open your letterhead file and click your pointer at the top of the page. Select *Paste* from the *Edit* menu. When your logo appears, highlight it and use the commands in the *Paragraph* menu (see page 61) to position it in the middle of your page, or on the left- or right-hand side. In a Write document, text can't appear on the same line as a picture.

Personal Cards

A great way to give people your address and telephone number is on a personal card. To make one, open a copy of Paintbrush. Select *Image Attributes...* in the *Options* menu and specify a

canvas that is about 9cm wide and 5.5cm high.

This is the icon for the Rectangle tool. Use it to draw a rectangle around the edge of your canvas to form an outline. Paste a copy of your logo onto the card using the technique described on page 70. Type in your address and phone number using the Text tool.

When you have finished, select *Save As...* in the *File* menu. Give your file a name, place it in the projects directory and save it.

Here is a sample card.

Fleur Smith
27 Long Street
Middletown

0191 456 876

Cards galore

By copying your personal card a number of times, you can produce a printed sheet of cards that you can cut out and give to your friends. Open the file containing your card and use the Pick tool to cut around it. Select *Copy* in the *Edit* menu.

This is the Pick tool icon.

Next, you need to create a new canvas to paste your card onto. Select *Image Attributes...* in the *Options* menu and create a canvas about 20 cm wide and 18cm high. When the canvas appears select *Zoom Out* in the *View* menu.

Your whole canvas will appear in the Paintbrush window. Select *Paste* in the *Edit* menu. A rectangle with crossed lines on it will appear. Click your pointer on the canvas outside this rectangle and a copy of your card will appear. If you select *Paste* again, a new rectangle will appear on top of your card. Click and drag this rectangle into position beside your first card.

Placing six cards onto a canvas

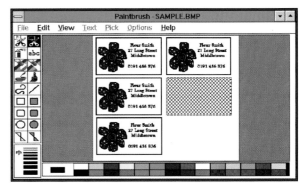

Repeat this process until you have six cards on your canvas. Now select *Zoom In* in the *View* menu. Select *Save As...* in the *File* menu. Give your file a new name (say, sixcard.bmp), place it in the projects directory and save it.

Printing out

Print out the file with your six cards onto a piece of paper. You can use colorful paper or use pens and paints to add color to your cards.

Glue the paper to a sheet of thin cardboard. When it is dry, carefully cut out the cards.

Decorate your card with pens, pencils or paints.

Outlines and stencils

With Paintbrush's Text tool you can create outlined letters. Print them out and color them in, or make them into stencils to decorate your possessions.

Outlined letters

To create outlined text, open a copy of Paintbrush and select the Text tool. In the *Text* menu, choose the font, size and style of the text you want to use. Also in the *Text* menu, select *Bold* and *Outline* so that check marks appear beside them.

Paintbrush's Text menu

Text	
Regular	
√ Bold	Ctrl+B
Italic	Ctrl+I
Underline	Ctrl+U
√ Outline	
Shadow	
Fonts...	

Choose white as your foreground color and black as your background color. Type in some outlined letters using the keyboard. When you have finished, change your background color to white and foreground color to black.

A sample of outlined text

Thicker letters

To make the outlines of your letters thicker, drag a rectangle around your letters with the Pick tool. Select *Copy* in the *Edit* menu and then select *Paste*. A copy of your letters will appear in the top left-hand corner of your canvas.

A copy of your lettering

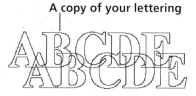

With your pointer, drag this copy almost exactly over the top of the other letters. You will see that when it is almost, but not quite, over the top, the letters look twice as thick. Release your mouse button to position the letters.

The copy is right beside the original.

If the letters of your text are too close together, use the Scissor tool to cut carefully around each one. Click on it, and drag it slightly away from its neighbor.

What is a stencil?

A stencil is a design that is cut into paper or plastic. You dab paint into the cutout shape to leave a pattern when the stencil is lifted off.

You can use outlined letters created in Paintbrush to make a stencil to decorate a folder, a pencil holder or a mug.

Some of the things you can decorate with stencils.

Making a stencil

First measure the size of the area you want to stencil. Open a copy of Paintbrush, and select *Image Attributes...* in the *Options* menu. Specify a canvas that is the same size as the area you want to stencil. Now, when you design your stencil, you will be able to see exactly how much of the object it will cover.

When you have finished your stencil design, select *Save As...* in the *File* menu. Give the file a filename (stencil.bmp for example), place it in your projects directory and save it.

Printing out

Print out your file onto the thickest paper you can use in your printer. Stencils get soggy when you use paint on them, so the thicker the paper, the longer they will last.

On this page, you can find out how to use a Paintbrush stencil to decorate the lid of a pencil holder.

Stenciling

To stencil the lid of a pencil holder, you will need the following things: a sponge or crumpled cloth, ceramic paints, a piece of clear book-covering film, masking tape, a pencil holder, a ruler and an old saucer.

This is what you do:

1. Measure the lid of your holder and specify a canvas in Paintbrush that is the same size as it. Type your name in outlined type.

This canvas is the same size as the holder's lid.

2. Print out your name onto paper. Cut a piece of book-covering film that is slightly smaller than the lid of the holder. Tape the film over the letters on your printout.

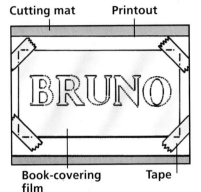

Cutting mat **Printout**

Book-covering film **Tape**

3. Using a craft knife, cut out all the letters. Make sure you cut through both the printout paper and the book-covering film.

Smooth out edges as you cut.

4. Separate the printout and the film and stick the film onto the holder. Add any middle parts of letters.

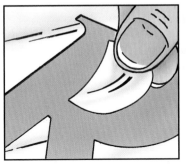

5. Put some paint onto the saucer. Dip the sponge into it, dab it on a paper towel, then over the letters.

6. Peel off the film carefully when the paint is dry.

All change

The Paintbrush application allows you to alter pictures by adding details to them and making them larger or smaller.

Dressing up

You can make different costumes for a figure drawn in Paintbrush. Open a copy of Paintbrush and draw a basic body shape. When you are ready, select *Save As...* in the *File* menu. Give your file a name (say, body.bmp), place it in your projects directory and save it.

A basic body shape in Paintbrush, ready to be altered

All change

Draw an outfit for your figure. Select *Save As...* in the *File* menu. Give your file a new name (such as clown.bmp) and place it in your projects directory. This ensures that your body.bmp file remains unaltered.

To design another outfit, select *Open...* in the *File* menu and highlight the body.bmp file in your projects directory. Click *OK* and your basic body will reappear.

Finishing touches

Print out your pictures onto paper. Glue thin pieces of cardboard to the back of the printouts. When the glue is dry, use a sharp pair of scissors or a craft knife to cut around your figures. If you don't have a color printer, use crayons or paints to color in the clothes.

To make a figure stand up, glue a triangular piece of cardboard to the back of it.

A selection of figures you could make

Badges

You can use Paintbrush to design a selection of badges. Try making the logo you drew on page 70 into a badge. To find your logo, open Paintbrush and in the *File Name* list, highlight your logo.bmp file in the projects directory and click *OK*. The file will open.

Draw around your logo with the Pick tool and select *Copy* in the *Edit* menu. Now select *New* in the *File* menu. When a new canvas appears on your screen select *Image Attributes...* in the *Options* menu. Click on the *Default* button and then select *OK*. Finally select *Paste* in the *Edit* menu and a copy of your logo will appear on the canvas.

Some badge designs based on logos

Shrink and grow

In your new Paintbrush file you can change the size and shape of your logo. With the Pick tool draw a rectangle around it. Select *Shrink + Grow* in the *Pick* menu. Your pointer will change into a cross-shaped cursor. Move it to a clear area of your canvas. Click the cursor on the canvas and drag a rectangular shape. When you release your mouse button, a copy of your logo will appear.

***Using* Shrink + <u>G</u>row**

A picture

To make the picture bigger, drag a large rectangle.

To shrink it, draw a small rectangle.

Undistorted

When you use *Shrink + Grow*, you can drag out a rectangle of any size and shape, and your logo will change to fill it. However, to make sure that your logo is not distorted (which means stretched too wide or too narrow), hold down the Shift key while you drag out the rectangle.

Making badges

When you are happy with the size and shape of the logo for your badge, select *Save As...* in the *File* menu. Give your file a name (say, badge.bmp) place it in the projects directory and save it.

Print out your badge file onto a piece of paper. Glue a piece of thin cardboard to the back of the paper. Cut out your badge and color it, as in the previous project.

To make your badge more hard-wearing, you could cover it with some clear book-covering film.

Use tape or a bandaid to attach a safety pin to the back of the badge.

These badges have been colored in with felt-tip pens.

Mouse mats

When using a computer mouse, you need to have a clean, flat surface to work on. You can buy a special mouse mat, or make your own using the Paintbrush application.

Here are some ideas for mouse mats to make.

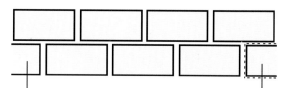

A graffiti mat

To create a mat with your name written on it like graffiti on a wall, open a copy of Paintbrush and maximize it to fill your screen. Select *Page Setup...* in the *File* menu. A dialog box appears. In the Margins section enter "0" for the *Top*, *Bottom*, *Left* and *Right* margins and click *OK*.

Select *Image Attributes...* in the *Options* menu and in the dialog box, specify a canvas 7cm wide and 10cm high. Then click *OK*.

Brick laying

Select the Rectangle tool and choose white as your foreground color and black as your background color. In the top left-hand corner of your canvas area draw a brick.

The Rectangle tool icon

Select the Roller tool and choose a pale color as your foreground color. Click the inside of your brick to fill it with paint.

The Roller tool icon

Creating a brick wall

To create a wall of bricks, use the Pick tool to cut around your brick. Select *Copy* in the *Edit* menu and then *Paste*. A new brick will appear on top left-hand corner of the canvas.

Drag the brick into position beside the first brick, with a small gap between them. Repeat this process until you have a full row of bricks.

Copying rows of bricks

When you select *Zoom Out* in the *View* menu, your whole canvas will appear in the Paintbrush window. Use the Pick tool to draw around the row of bricks. Select *Copy* in the *Edit* menu and then select *Paste*.

A block covered with crossed lines will appear. Drag this box underneath your first row of bricks. When it is in position, click your cursor on the canvas outside the block. A new row of bricks will appear.

Select *Paste* again for another row of bricks to position and gradually fill your canvas with rows of bricks.

Copying a row of bricks

Move the new row of bricks across half a brick.

Copy and paste half a brick into the space at the end of each row.

Writing on the wall

Select a wide width in the Line Width box and, with the Eraser tool, write your name across the wall. Add any decoration you like. Select *Save As...* in the *File* menu. Give your file a name, place it in the projects directory and save it.

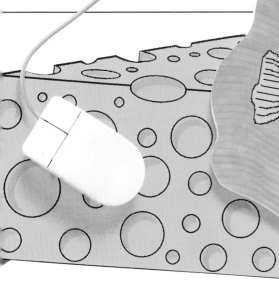

A cheese mat

To make a cheese mat, open a copy of Paintbrush. Specify a canvas in the same way as described for the graffiti mat.

Use the Rectangle tool to draw a rectangle like the one in the picture below.

 This is the icon for the Line tool. Use it to draw a line to form the top edge of the cheese.

Select the Curve Line tool icon and draw a line joining the top of the cheese to the rectangle. Use your cursor to curve the line. This is difficult. If you go wrong, select *Undo* in the *Edit* menu.

This is what the finished cheese will look like.

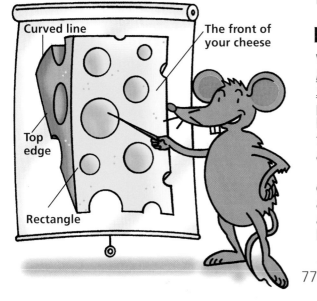

Curved line

The front of your cheese

Top edge

Rectangle

Lots of holes

Use the Circle tool to draw holes in your cheese. The holes on the front of the cheese should be perfect circles. If you hold down the Shift key while you drag, you will get a circle. The holes on the top of the cheese should be squashed circles, called ellipses. You can draw them by dragging wide circles with your cursor.

An ellipse

A circle

On the edge

Make sure that some of the circles you draw extend over the edge of the cheese. Where they fall outside the cheese, use the Eraser tool to rub out part of the circle and the edge.

Finishing touches

When your picture is ready, select *Print...* in the *File* menu. In the Print box specify 275% in the *Scaling* section. Print the file onto a piece of A4 paper (about 8 inches wide and 11.5 inches high). You could use a sheet of yellow paper for the cheese mat. Use paints to add color to the printout.

Finally, glue the printout onto a piece of cardboard and cover both cardboard and printout in clear book-covering film.

Stickers and scenes

An aquarium filled with exotic fish, Photofit faces and fabulous fashion, are just some of the things you can create with a technique called clip-art. You will need to use the Paintbrush application.

What is clip-art

Clip-art is a method of transferring a set of pictures from one Paintbrush window to another. You can treat the pictures like reusable stickers, sticking them onto different scenes and using them in different combinations.

Two copies of Paintbrush

To tackle a clip-art project, you need two copies of Paintbrush open at once. First, open one copy of Paintbrush by double-clicking on its icon in Program Manager. Use your cursor to resize (see page 53) this window until it covers the top half of your screen.

Go back to Program Manager and open another copy of Paintbrush by double-clicking on its icon again. Resize this window to fill the bottom half of your screen.

Active window

When you have two copies of the Paintbrush window open, click on the window you want to work on and it will become active, which means it is ready to use. The other window, which is not being used, is called inactive.

Making stickers

Maximize one of the Paintbrush windows to fill your screen. Draw a selection of pictures, say a group of fish. This will be your stickers canvas.

A selection of stickers

Make sure the stickers are small, so that they can fit into a scene.

When you have finished, select *Save As...* in the *File* menu, give this Paintbrush file a name, place it in the projects directory and save it. Click the Restore button of this Paintbrush window.

Setting a scene

Now create a scene for your stickers to appear in. Maximize your second Paintbrush window. Make sure that the background color you select for this canvas is the same as that chosen for your stickers canvas. Design a scene.

This is your scenery canvas. Select *Save As...* in the *File* menu, give the file a name, place it in the projects directory and save it. Click the Restore button of this Paintbrush window.

An aquarium scene

Copying and pasting

 This is the icon for the Scissor tool. Use it to draw around one of the pictures on your stickers canvas. Select *Copy* in the *Edit* menu. In your scenery canvas, click the Maximize button and select *Paste* in the *Edit* menu. The sticker will appear on your canvas.

Click on the sticker and drag it where you want it. Then release the mouse button. Once you click anywhere outside the dotted line around your sticker, you won't be able to move it again.

Move your stickers into position in your scene.

All change

You can vary the size of your stickers, as in the picture above, by using the "Shrink and grow" technique described on page 75.

To make a sticker point in another direction, draw around it with the Pick tool and select *Flip Horizontal* or *Flip Vertical* in the *Pick* menu.

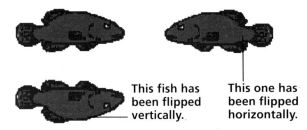

This fish has been flipped vertically.   **This one has been flipped horizontally.**

When your clip-art picture is finished, select *Save As...* in the *File* menu, give the file a name, place it in the projects directory and save it.

More clip-art ideas

You can use clip-art in many different ways. Try producing disguises by adding a selection of hair, glasses and beard stickers to a basic face. Create your own alphabet or design a variety of outfits and accessories to mix and match on a model.

You can create a rogues gallery of criminals.   ***Design your own alphabet.***

Design outfits with clip-art.

A picture address book

Using an application called Cardfile, you can create an address book to store on your computer. Add fun cartoon portraits of your friends to the cards, so that you laugh every time you look at them.

What is Cardfile?

Cardfile works like a pile of index cards that always remain stacked in alphabetical order. Open Cardfile by double-clicking on its icon in Program Manager.

This is the Cardfile icon.

A Cardfile window appears with "(Untitled)" in its Title bar. The window contains one index card, as shown below:

This is a Cardfile window.

The Index Line

The main area of the card

It's a good idea to give your new cardfile a name right away. Select *Save As...* in the *File* menu. Give your file a filename with a .CRD extension. Place it in your projects directory and save it.

Filling the cards

To use the first card that appears when Cardfile opens, double-click in the Index Line area. An Index dialog box opens.

An Index dialog box

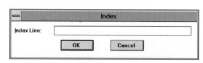

Type the name of one of your friends in the *Index Line* box. Put their last name first, because address books are usually arranged in alphabetical order according to last name. Then click *OK*.

To add an address and a telephone number, click in the main area of the card. A flashing cursor will appear and you can start typing.

Adding cards

To add a new card for each of your friends, press the F7 key. In the Index dialog box, type in another friend's name and click *OK*. A new card will appear at the top of your pile.

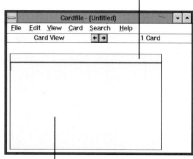

Face facts

Pictures added to the index cards will make your address book more colorful. Alternatively, you could add a map showing you how to find a friend's house.

You can draw pictures using Paintbrush and then paste them onto your address cards using the technique below.

Sizing

To prepare a canvas that is the correct size for your picture, minimize the Cardfile window. Open a copy of Paintbrush by double-clicking on its icon. In the *Options* menu select *Image Attributes...*

In the dialog box that appears, make sure that you are working in centimeters by selecting cm in the *Units* section. Enter a size of about 6cm in the width box and 6cm in the height box. Then click *OK* and close that copy of Paintbrush by double-clicking in its control-menu box.

Creating a picture

Return to your Cardfile window by double-clicking on its icon at the foot of your screen. Choose the card of one of your friends. Bring it to the front of the pile by clicking on its Index Line. You can also use the arrows below the Cardfile Menu bar to flick through your cards. This is what the arrows look like.

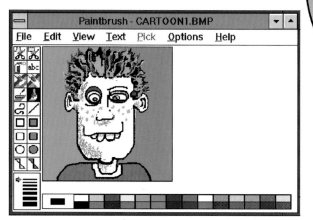

To add a picture to the card, open the *Edit* menu and select *Picture*. Now, click on *Insert Object...* in the *Edit* menu and a dialog box similar to the one below will appear.

An Insert New Object dialog box

Select *Paintbrush Picture* in the *Object Type* list. When you click *OK,* a Paintbrush window will open containing a correctly sized canvas. Now you are ready to draw a picture.

A cartoon picture on a canvas in Paintbrush

Inserting a picture

When you have completed your picture, select *Update* in Paintbrush's *File* menu. Click on *Exit & Return to...* in the *File* menu. The picture will appear on your index card. Drag it into position.

Each card can have an address and a picture.

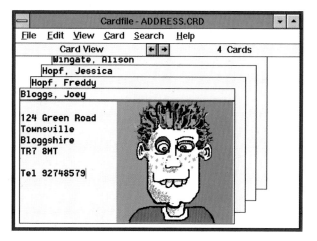

All change

It's easy to alter an index card if one of your friends moves home or even grows a beard. To change text, select *Text* in Cardfile's *Edit* menu. Alter the name at the top of a card by double-clicking in the Index Line area. A dialog box appears. Make your changes and click *OK*. To alter an address, click in the main area of the card and type in your changes.

To change a picture, select *Picture* in the *Edit* menu. Double-click on the picture you want to alter and a copy of Paintbrush will open. When you have made your alterations, click on *Update* in the *File* menu. Finally, Click on *Exit and Return to...* in the *File* menu.

Whenever you add a new card to your cardfile or change an existing card, save the cardfile before closing it. To do this, select *Save* in the *File* menu.

Character maps and codes

You can use your computer to send baffling, coded messages. People won't be able to understand these messages until you explain how to decode them using a Windows application called Character Map.

What is a character?

Any letter, number or symbol that your computer can produce is called a character. Each font (see page 62) has up to 256 different characters. This book is printed in a font called Frutiger 45. So, 3, m, @ and # are all characters in that particular font.

Character Maps

This is the icon for the Character Map application. When you open it, by double-clicking on the icon in Program Manager, a

window like the one below appears. It contains a map of all the characters available in one of the fonts stored on your computer.

There are different maps for each of the fonts. To look at

the different maps, open the *Font* list and highlight the name of another font. The character map will change to show all the characters available in that particular font.

This is the Character Map window showing the map of a font called Times.

This is the name of the font to which all the characters in this map belong.

In this window appears a list of any characters you select.

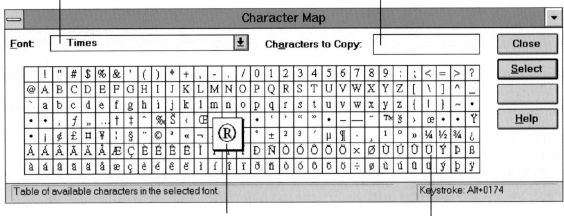

This character has been magnified using the pointer.

Each square contains a different character.

A closer look

The character map squares are very small and it can be difficult to see the exact shape of some of the characters. To take a closer look at any character in the map, click on its square and hold down your mouse button. As you click, the square will appear magnified.

Coded messages

To write a coded message, open a copy of Write by double-clicking on its icon in Program Manager. In the *Character* menu select *Fonts...* Select the font called Arial and click *OK*.

Now type into your Write document the secret message you want to send.

Use the cursor to highlight your message. Select *Fonts...* in the *Character* menu again and choose the font called Symbol. Symbol has lots of strange characters.

This is a coded message in Symbol. Find out how to decode it below.

Αγεντ Τινκερβελλ
Χομε ανδ φινδ με
ουτσιδε Πηαραον
Τυτ σ πψραμιδ ατ
μιδνιγητ τονιγητ.
Ι ωιλλ βε δισγυισεδ
ασ α χαμελ οωνερ.
Τηε πασσωορδ ισ
Οκλαηομα.
Σιγνεδ

Αγεντ Οβϖιουσ

To make sure that your message is large enough to read easily when it is printed out, select 14 in the *Size* list in the Fonts dialog box.

Now choose *OK* and your message will be instantly transformed into a mysterious collection of symbols.

Sending your message

To save your message, select *Save As...* in the *File* menu. Give your file a name, place it in the projects directory and save it. Print out this file onto a piece of paper and send it to a friend. Close the Write window by double-clicking in its control menu box.

Remember, your friend must have a computer that has Windows software installed, in order to translate your message.

Tell your friend

Let your friend try and figure out the code for a while, but then reveal some clues about how to decode it.

Say that your message is written in Symbol and that using the Character Map application is the only way to decipher it.

Time to decode

This is what your friend needs to do to decode the message. Open Character Map and select Symbol in the *Font* list. Starting with the first character in your message, use the pointer to move around the map, looking for a character that exactly matches the one in your message.

When your friend finds the right character, he or she should double-click on the square in which the character appears. The symbol will appear in the *Character to Copy* box, like the one below.

Characters to Copy: Αγεντ Οβϖιουσ

Your friend should work through in this way, not forgetting to put in spaces where they appear in your message.

All is revealed

At the end of the message, your friend should click the *Copy* button. Close Character Map by double-clicking in its control menu box and open a copy of Write. Select *Fonts...* in the *Character* menu. In the *Font* list select the font called Arial and click *OK*. Finally, open Write's *Edit* menu and select *Paste*.

Your message will appear in the Write document decoded and ready to read.

Invent your own quiz game

You can create a Cardfile with quiz questions on each index card. Using an application called Object Packager, you can hide the answers on the cards. When you want to reveal an answer, all you have to do is double-click.

A quiz question on an index card

```
QUESTION 1

WHAT IS THE CAPITAL CITY OF FRANCE?
```

What is Object Packager?

This is the icon for Object Packager. This application "packages" up one file and inserts it into another. The file that is packaged up is called the object. It can be any kind of file, like a Paintbrush picture or a Write document. The file into which the object is inserted is called the destination file.

The object file appears in the destination file as an icon. When you double-click on this icon the object file automatically opens.

Questions and answers

To produce a quiz game, start by thinking up a selection of questions and answers. Following the instructions on page 80, create a Cardfile, give it a filename, place it in your projects directory and save it.

Open Cardfile's *Edit* menu and click on *Text*. On your first index card, type a number on the Index Line and a question on the main area of the card. Then minimize Cardfile.

Open a copy of Write and type in the answer to your question. Select *Save As...* in the *File* menu. Give your file a filename (answer1.wri for example), place it in your projects directory and save it.

Packaging an object

Now you need to package up the answer document and insert it into your index card. Open Object Packager by double-clicking on its icon in Program Manager. In the window, click on the word Content. Select *Import...* in the *File* menu. In the dialog box that opens, highlight answer1.wri in your projects directory and click *OK*.

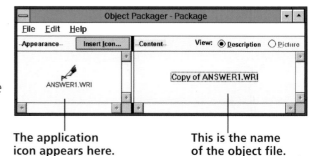

The filename appears in the Content section of Object Packager's window and a Write icon appears in the Appearance section. Select *Copy Package* in the *Edit* menu and then close Object Packager by double-clicking in its control-menu box.

This is Object Packager's window containing a packaged Write file.

```
─                Object Packager - Package            ▼ ▲
 File   Edit   Help
─Appearance─    Insert Icon...    ─Content─   View: ● Description  ○ Picture

                                          Copy of ANSWER1.WRI

        ANSWER1.WRI
```

The application icon appears here.   **This is the name of the object file.**

Inserting an object

To insert an answer document into an index card, first maximize the Cardfile window. Open the *Edit* menu, select *Picture* so that a check mark appears. Select *Paste* in the *Edit* menu. A Write icon appears. Drag it into position.

To find out the answer to the question on the card, double-click on this icon. The Write document containing the answer opens. Close it when you have finished by double-clicking in its control-menu box. Repeat this process to add more question cards and answers to your cardfile.

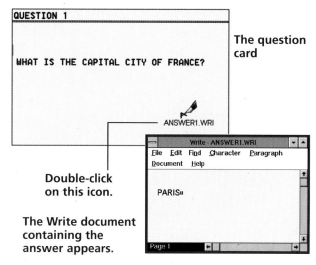

An index card with a Write file packaged in it

QUESTION 1

WHAT IS THE CAPITAL CITY OF FRANCE?

ANSWER1.WRI

The question card

Double-click on this icon.

The Write document containing the answer appears.

Write - ANSWER1.WRI

File   Edit   Find   Character   Paragraph
Document   Help

PARIS¤

Page 1

Computer sound

Many computers can make sounds. Find out if your computer can by opening Control Panel. Double-click on the Sound icon.

 This is the Sound icon.

In the dialog box that opens, there is a list of sound files. They have the filename extension .WAV.

If the files listed in the *Files* section appear dimmed (pale grey), it means that your computer can't make sounds. If they aren't dimmed, highlight one of them and click the *Test* button. You should hear a sound. If you do, you can use some of these sound files in your quiz game.

The Sound window with a list of .WAV files

Sound
Events:	Files:
Asterisk	applause.wav	OK
Critical Stop	boing.wav	Cancel
Default Beep	boingboi.wav	
Exclamation	bomb.wav	Test
Question	chimes.wav	
Windows Exit	chord.wav	Help
Windows Start	creak.wav	
	ding.wav	
☒ Enable System Sounds	c:\windows	

Adding sounds

Open Object Packager and select *Import...* in the *File* menu. In the dialog box that appears, select the directory called windows. In the File *Name* box, type *.WAV and press the Return key. A list of the .WAV files on your computer appears. You may have one called applause.wav. Highlight it in the File *Name* list, then click *OK*. If you don't have this file, choose another one. Finally, select *Copy Package* in the *Edit* menu.

Close Object Packager and open your cardfile. Double-click on the Write icon on one of your cards to open an answer file. When it appears, position your cursor at the end of the text and select *Paste* in the *Edit* menu. A Sound icon will appear. Select *Save* in the *File* menu to ensure that the Sound file is saved in your Write file.

Now, if you get the answer right, double-click on this Sound icon and you will hear a round of applause.

Finding a hidden message

Using Object Packager, you can hide a secret file in an innocent-looking letter. Only your friends will know how to reveal the hidden information.

The picture at the bottom of the letter below looks pretty innocent. But when you double-click on it, a Paintbrush file opens revealing a less flattering portrait.

Double-clicking on the picture above opens this hidden Paintbrush file.

An innocent letter

First, you need to create a letter in which to hide a secret file. Open Write by double-clicking on its icon in Program Manager. In the Write window, type a letter. When you have finished, minimize the Write window so that it appears as an icon at the bottom of your screen.

Compiling a secret file

Next, open Paintbrush and draw a secret picture. When you have finished, select *Save As...* in the *File* menu. Give your file a name (say, secret.bmp), place it in your projects directory and save it. Close Paintbrush by double-clicking in its control-menu box.

Packaging secrets

Open Object Packager and click on the Content section. Select *Import...* in the *File* menu. In the dialog box that appears, highlight the secret information file (secret.bmp) in your projects directory. When you click *OK*, the filename will appear in the Content section and a Paintbrush icon in the Appearance section.

Creating a disguise

Next, you need to disguise the icon in which your secret document is packaged. Click on the Object Packager's Appearance section and select *Cut* in the *Edit* menu. Minimize Object Packager and open a new copy of Paintbrush. Select *Paste* in the *Edit* menu. The icon from the Appearance section will appear on your canvas. Use the Eraser tool to erase it.

In its place, draw an innocent-looking picture that will fit on your letter. Then, using the Scissor tool, cut around it. Select *Copy* in the *Edit* menu.

Close Paintbrush by double-clicking in its control-menu box. You don't need to save this file.

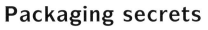

Hiding the evidence

Maximize Object Packager, and select *Paste* in the *Edit* menu. Your secret picture will appear in the Appearance section. Select *Copy Pac*k*age* in the *Edit* menu and close Object Packager by double-clicking in its control-menu box.

The Paintbrush icon is replaced by your picture in Object Packager.

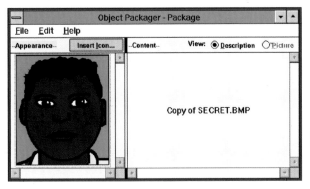

Maximize the Write file containing your letter. Place your cursor at the bottom of the text. Then select *Paste* in the *Edit* menu and the picture will appear.

To save the letter and the hidden file, select *Save As...* in Write's *File* menu. Give your file a name (say letter1.wri), place it in your projects directory and save it.

All is revealed

To reveal the hidden file, all you need to do is double-click on the picture at the bottom of your letter. The Paintbrush file containing your secret picture will open automatically. To close it, double-click in its control-menu box.

Sending your letter

To send this letter to a friend, copy the letter1.wri file onto a floppy disk. To do this, put a floppy disk in your computer's floppy disk drive. Open File Manager, which has an icon like this.

Close all but one of the windows inside the File Manager window. Select *Select Drive...* in the *Disk* menu and in the dialog box that appears select the hard disk drive (usually labeled as the C drive).

A list of the directories on your hard disk will appear in the left-hand side of the window. Find your projects directory and double-click on it.

A list will appear in the right-hand side of the window. Click on your letter1.wri and drag it over to the symbol in the top left-hand corner of the window that looks like this.

This is your floppy disk drive. Release the mouse button. To check that your file has been copied onto the floppy disk, click your pointer on this symbol once. The name of your file will appear in the right-hand side of the window.

Who does this belong to?

You could set up a picture like the one below. Each character has a picture hidden in it. When you double-click on each character, you can find out who the tutu belongs to.

Double-click here   Double-click here

Unlikely!

That's more like it.

Interactive storytime

Most stories have a beginning, a middle, and an end. Their plots never change. But with an "interactive" story, you can decide what happens next by making a series of choices. An interactive story has several possible plots and endings. Using Cardfile, you can write a story that will be different every time you read it.

Make sure that *Picture* is selected in the *Edit* menu and then select *Paste* in the *Edit* menu. When your picture appears, drag it to position.

Planning your story

To get an idea of how an interactive story works, look at the example on page 89. You need to create a series of index cards, each containing an event and two possible courses of action. Depending on which course you choose, you are directed to another numbered card, where the story continues. By making choices in this way, the plot develops.

Interactive stories are difficult to write, so plan your story first. You can make it as complex as you like, with as many cards and choices as you like. Make sure, however, that you include a selection of cards with different endings to your story.

Adding sounds

If your computer can make sounds (see page 85), you can use Object Packager to add sound files to your index cards. Follow the technique described on page 85.

To increase the number of sound files you have to choose from, you can use a piece of software called the Microsoft® Sound Driver. It is a floppy disk that holds a selection of sound files which you can copy onto your computer.

Jumping between cards

To move from one card to another, click on the Index Line of the card you want. Alternatively, press the F4 key on the top row of your keyboard. A dialog box appears. Type in the number of the card you require and click *OK*. That card will jump to the top of your pile.

Creating a story cardfile

To find out how to create a cardfile, look at page 80. Give each index card a number on its Index Line and add the events and choices in your story to the main area of the card.

You can add pictures to some of your cards if you like. To do this, open a copy of Paintbrush. Draw a picture and select the Pick tool to cut it out.

Select *Cut* in the *Edit* menu, and then close Paintbrush without saving the file. Open your Cardfile and click on the card that you want to paste your picture onto.

This is the Go To dialog box.

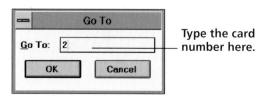

Type the card number here.

Playing the game

When you are ready to read your story, make sure *Picture* has a check mark beside it in Cardfile's *Edit* menu. This will ensure that when you double-click on a Sound icon on a card you will be able to hear the sound file play.

The story below is short and simple. You could set up an identical cardfile to give yourself an idea of how an interactive story works.

When you have written your own interactive story get people to read it. Watch them make choices. Were they the same as yours? They could even write some new index cards themselves to add a whole set of new adventures to the story.

These are some index cards that make up an interactive story.

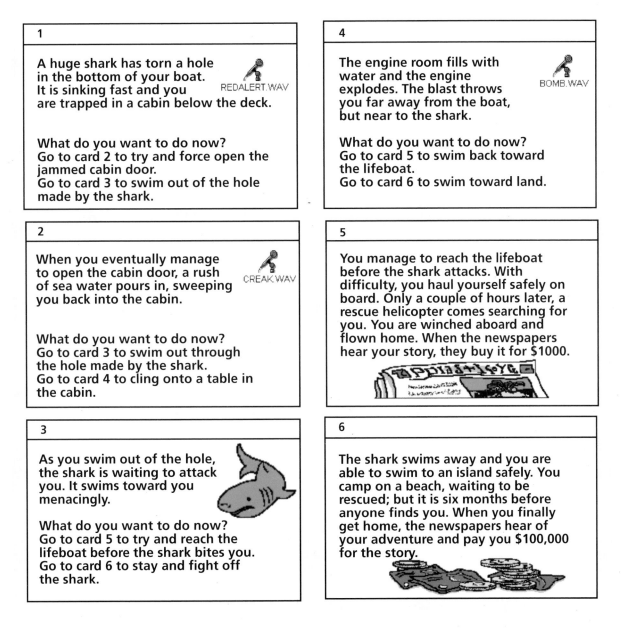

1

A huge shark has torn a hole in the bottom of your boat. It is sinking fast and you are trapped in a cabin below the deck.

REDALERT.WAV

What do you want to do now?
Go to card 2 to try and force open the jammed cabin door.
Go to card 3 to swim out of the hole made by the shark.

2

When you eventually manage to open the cabin door, a rush of sea water pours in, sweeping you back into the cabin.

CREAK.WAV

What do you want to do now?
Go to card 3 to swim out through the hole made by the shark.
Go to card 4 to cling onto a table in the cabin.

3

As you swim out of the hole, the shark is waiting to attack you. It swims toward you menacingly.

What do you want to do now?
Go to card 5 to try and reach the lifeboat before the shark bites you.
Go to card 6 to stay and fight off the shark.

4

The engine room fills with water and the engine explodes. The blast throws you far away from the boat, but near to the shark.

BOMB.WAV

What do you want to do now?
Go to card 5 to swim back toward the lifeboat.
Go to card 6 to swim toward land.

5

You manage to reach the lifeboat before the shark attacks. With difficulty, you haul yourself safely on board. Only a couple of hours later, a rescue helicopter comes searching for you. You are winched aboard and flown home. When the newspapers hear your story, they buy it for $1000.

6

The shark swims away and you are able to swim to an island safely. You camp on a beach, waiting to be rescued; but it is six months before anyone finds you. When you finally get home, the newspapers hear of your adventure and pay you $100,000 for the story.

Macro magic

You can use an application called Recorder to record yourself drawing a picture in Paintbrush. Then watch as the picture magically redraws itself when you play back the recording. Recorder is a difficult application to use, so follow the instructions for this project carefully.

What is Recorder?

Recorder records the movements of your mouse and any keys that you press. It then plays back these actions. A recorded set of mouse movements and keystrokes is called a macro.

This is the icon for Recorder.

You can use Recorder like a video recorder. By recording the way in which a picture is drawn, Recorder can redraw the picture by playing back the recorded actions.

Preparations

To record yourself drawing a picture, open Paintbrush by double-clicking on its icon in Program Manager. Size the Paintbrush window to fill the top three-quarters of your screen. Select the Brush tool in the Toolbox. Make sure that the background color selected is white and the foreground color is black. Finally, minimize Paintbrush.

Using Recorder

In Program Manager, find the Recorder icon and double-click on it. When the Recorder window opens, select *Record...* in the *Macro* menu. In the dialog box that appears, make the same selections as shown in the following sample Record Macro dialog box.

A Record Macro dialog box

Give your macro a name here.

No cross in the *Continuous Loop* check box.

In the *Playback* section select *Fast*.

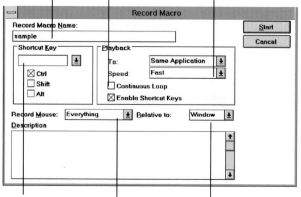

Leave this section blank.

In the *Record Mouse* section select *Everything*.

In the *Relative to* menu select *Window*.

Recording a macro

When you have entered these preferences, click the *Start* button. A flashing Recorder icon will appear at the bottom of your screen. This tells you that Recorder is recording. Double-click on the Paintbrush icon at the bottom of your screen and start to draw your picture.

Simple patterns can look very effective.

Stop recording

To stop your recording when you have finished your picture, click once on the Recorder icon at the foot of your screen.

A Recorder dialog box will appear like the one below. Select *Save Macro* and then click *OK*.

This is the Recorder dialog box.

Preparing for playback

Recorder records the exact position of your pointer on screen. So before you play back a macro, make sure that all the objects on your screen are in the same position as they were before the macro was recorded. If you record a macro and then move, resize or close windows, it won't play back.

In Paintbrush, make sure that the Brush tool is highlighted and that the background selected color is white and the foreground color is black.

Select *New...* in Paintbrush's *File* menu. A dialog box will appear asking "Do you want to save current changes?". Choose *No*. When a new canvas appears, minimize the Paintbrush window.

Playing a macro

To play back your macro, double-click on the Recorder icon. In the Recorder box, highlight the name of your macro and select *Run* in the *Macro* menu. Watch while your picture redraws itself.

Speed

You can play back a macro at two different speeds: fast or at the speed at which you recorded it.

To alter the speed, you have to change the selection in the *Playback* section of the Record Marco box before you record a new macro.

Saving macros

When you have recorded some macros, you can save them all in one file. Select *Save As...* in Recorder's *File* menu. Give your file a filename and a .REC extension. Finally, place it in the projects directory and save it.

Guessing games

There are lots of ways to use Recorder. Try playing the game below. In Recorder, select *Record...* in the *Macro* menu. In the dialog box, choose *Recorded Speed* in the *Playback* section.

Record a macro of drawing a picture. When you play it back, get your friends to try to guess what the picture is before it is complete.

A picture is revealed.

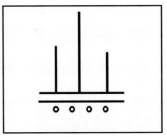

Can you guess what it is?

Now can you guess?

So that's what it is!

Cartoon fun

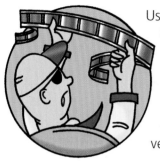

Using the Recorder application and a technique called clip-art, you can produce a simple but effective cartoon. This is a difficult project, so don't worry if you take some time to get it right. Follow the stages described below very carefully.

Scenes and characters

To prepare your cartoon, you need to draw a scene for the action to take place in, and a "character" to move around the scene.

Following the clip-art technique described on pages 78 and 79, open two copies of Paintbrush. Draw a scene on one canvas and a character on the other. Give each picture a different filename (say, scene.bmp and charcter.bmp). Place them both in your projects directory and save them.

This scenery canvas has an outer space setting with stars and planets.

This rocket is the character that will travel through the space scene.

Maximize the Paintbrush window containing your character. Use the Scissor tool to cut around it. Select _Copy_ in the _Edit_ menu. Now double-click in the control-menu box to close this window.

Making preparations

Resize you scenery canvas to fill the top three-quarters of your screen. Click on its Minimize button, so that it appears as an icon at the foot of your screen. This will ensure that when you restore this Paintbrush window, when you are recording your macro (see page 90), you have plenty of space to work in.

Setting up your recording

Open Recorder by double-clicking on its icon in Program Manager. Select _Record..._ in the _Macro_ menu. In the dialog box that appears, make the same selections as in the box shown on page 90. You could, however, select _Recorded Speed_ in the _Playback_ section, which is a better speed for playing back cartoons.

Shortcut keys

In the Record Macro dialog box there is a section called _Shortcut Key_. You can choose a code of two keys that, when pressed together, will automatically play back your macro.

If you want to use a shortcut key code, click in the box beside _Enable Shortcut Keys_ until a cross appears. In the _Shortcut Key_ box select a key from the drop-down list (say, F4). Next, place a cross in one of the boxes beside Ctrl, Shift or Alt (Ctrl, for example). This is your code.

The Shortcut Key and the Playback sections in the Record Macro dialog box

Shortcut Key		Playback	
F4 ±		To:	Same Application ±
☒ Ctrl		Speed:	Recorded Speed ±
☐ Shift		☐ Continuous Loop	
☐ Alt		☒ Enable Shortcut Keys	

Recording your cartoon

To start recording your cartoon, click on *Start* in the Record Macro box. Double-click on the Paintbrush logo at the bottom of your screen and your scenery canvas will open.

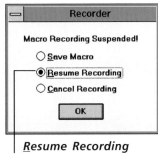

Select *Paste* in the *File* menu and a copy of your character will appear in your scene. Drag it around your scene, to give the impression of the character moving.

You can move other characters in your scene. Cut them out and drag them. Be careful that you don't cut out part of the background too, or this will move around with your character.

Click on the Recorder icon at the bottom of your screen. The Recorder dialog box will appear. If you want to stop your recording completely, select *Save Macro* and click *OK*.

Resuming your recording

If you don't want to stop recording, but you want to have time to think about where to move a character next, you can just pause your recording. To do this, click on the Recorder icon.

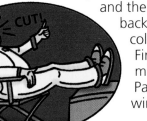

When you are ready to continue recording, select *Resume Recording* in the Recorder dialog box and then click *OK*.

The Recorder dialog box

Resume Recording is selected.

Preparing for playback

Remember, before you play back your macro you must put everything back into the position it was in when you started recording.

Select *Open...* in the *File* menu of your scenery Paintbrush window. A box will appear asking you "Do you want to save current changes?". Select *No*. An Open dialog box appears. Highlight the name of your scenery file (scene.bmp) in the *File Name* menu and then click *OK*. Your scenery canvas will reopen, looking as it did before you started recording.

Make sure that the Brush tool is selected and that the foreground color is black and the background color is white. Finally, minimize your Paintbrush window.

A cartoon masterpiece

To play back your cartoon, hold down your two shortcut keys.

The following screens show another idea for a cartoon sequence:

Cut around the bee with the Scissor tool and drag it around.

Make the bee bob from flower to flower.

Leave the bee, paste in a butterfly and float it around the flowers.

Windows® 95

You can read about a version of Windows called Windows® 95 on pages 46 and 47. If you have this software installed on your computer, you can still complete many of the projects. These pages tell you about some of the differences between Windows 95 and Windows 3.1, the version used in this book.

Starting Windows 95

When you switch on your computer and run the Windows 95 software, Program Manager doesn't appear on your screen. Instead a screen appears which includes a bar called a Taskbar. It contains a *Start* button like the one below.

Finding a program

To find a program stored on your computer, click the *Start* button. In the menu that appears, select *Programs*. Another menu will appear listing the program groups.

As you pass your pointer over the names of the program groups, further menus will open up, showing a list of the programs they contain.

Look through each group until you find the program you require.

*The **Start** menu and the Programs menu are open.*

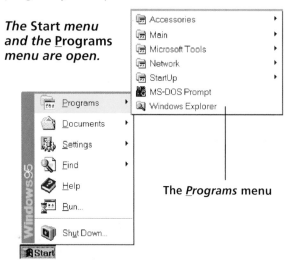

The *Programs* menu

Opening and closing programs

To open a program, double-click on its name in the menu. It will open in a window on your desktop. To close a program, select *Exit* in its *File* menu, or click once on the Close button in the top right-hand corner of the window.

A Windows 95 window

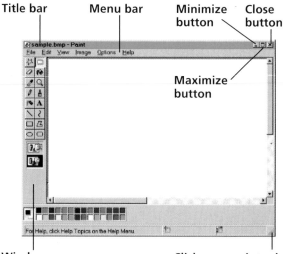

Title bar   Menu bar   Minimize button   Close button

Maximize button

Window   Click your pointer here to resize the window.

Switching between programs

Whenever you open a program in Windows 95, a new button representing that program appears on the Taskbar.

To switch from one open program to another, simply click on the button of the program you require. Its window will appear on top of your desktop.

The Taskbar showing two program buttons

| Start | letter1.doc - WordPad | picture4.bmp - Paint |

Opening and saving files

In Windows 95, the dialog boxes for opening and saving files are different from those in Windows 3.1; but they work in a similar way.

For example, the picture shows a *Save As* dialog box. Type in a name for your file in the *File name* box. Select the type of file you want it stored as in the *Save as type* box. To choose the directory you are going to save your file in, open the *Save in* list, click the disk drive you require, and then double-click on the folder you want to save your file in. When you have done this, click the *Save* button.

A Windows 95 Save As dialog box

Programs and icons

Many of the applications used in this book are included in Windows 95. Some, such as Character Map and Cardfile, are exactly the same as in Windows 3.1.

Write is replaced by an application called WordPad. The WordPad window includes a Toolbar which allows you to perform certain tasks quickly, like changing type styles and cutting and pasting text.

This is the WordPad icon.

Paintbrush is replaced by Paint. Its window is quite similar and has a Toolbox and Palette that enable you to draw pictures.

This is the Paint icon.

The Display dialog box has four sections. Appearance contains a sample window display for changing your color scheme (see pages 54 and 55). The Background section includes Desktop and Wallpaper (see pages 56 and 57, 66 and 67). Screensaver allows you to alter the screen savers on your computer (see pages 58 and 59).

The Display dialog box

Click on these labels to open a new folder.

Personalizing

You can still use Control Panel to personalize your display with pictures, patterns and colors. Click the *Start* button and select *Settings*. In the menu that appears click on Control Panel. The icon you need is the Display program shown here.

Not included

The Recorder and Object Packager applications don't appear in Windows 95. This means that you will be unable to tackle the projects in which these applications are required.

THE END

Index

First published in 1996 by Usborne Publishing Ltd, Usborne House, 83-85 Saffron Hill London EC1N 8RT, England.
Copyright © 1996 Usborne Publishing Ltd. The name Usborne and the device 🌐 are trade marks of Usborne Publishing Ltd.
All rights reserved. No part of this publication may be reproduced, stored in a retrieval system or transmitted in any form or by any means, electronic, mechanical, photocopying, recording or otherwise, without the prior permission of the publisher. AE.
First printed in America March 1997.
Printed in Spain.